HOW THINGS WORK

A SIMON AND SCHUSTER
color illustrated question and answer book

HOW THINGS WORK

A guide to how human-made and
living things function

Simon and Schuster Books for Young Readers
Published by Simon & Schuster Inc., New York

First American Edition, 1984
First published in 1983 by Kingfisher Books Limited
Elsley Court, 20-22 Great Titchfield Street
London W1P 7AD

Published by Simon and Schuster
Books for Young Readers
A Division of Simon & Schuster, Inc.
Simon & Schuster Building
1230 Avenue of the Americas
New York, New York 10020

10 9 8 7 6 5 4 3   10 9 8 7 6 5 4 3   (Pbk)

Simon and Schuster Books for Young Readers and colophon are
trademarks of Simon & Schuster, Inc.

Library of Congress Cataloging–in–Publication Data

Question & answer encyclopedia
    How things work/[authors, Neil Ardley...et al.; artists,
Bob Bampton...et al.].
    p. cm.–(A Simon & Schuster color illustrated question and
answer book)
    Reprint. Originally published: How Does It Work? London:
Kingfisher Books, 1983.
    Includes index.
    SUMMARY: Answers questions about how things work, from
appliances to scientific instruments to parts of the human body.
    1. Science–Miscellanea–Juvenile literature. 2. Technology–
Miscellanea–Juvenile literature. [1. Science–Miscellanea.
2. Questions and answers.] I. Ardley, Neil. II. Bampton, Bob, ill.
III. Title. IV. Series: Simon & Schuster color illustrated question &
answer book.
Q163.Q47 1988
500-dc 19
ISBN 0-671-67032-8 (Pbk)
ISBN 0-671-49898-3 ISBN 0-671-49992-0 (lib. bdg.)
                                                        88-1839
                                                           CIP
                                                            AC

Phototypeset by Southern Positives and Negatives
(SPAN) Lingfield, Surrey
Color separations by Newsele Litho Ltd,
Milan, Italy
Printed in Spain by Artes Graficas Toledo S.A.
D.L.TO:592-1991

Previously titled in the United Kingdom as
"How Does It Work?"

Authors
Neil Ardley
Mark Lambert
Christopher Maynard
James Muirden
Christopher Pick
Jill Wright

Artists
Dave Etchell & John Ridyard
Ron Jobson/Tudor Art Agency
Bernard Robinson/Tudor Art Agency
Mike Roffe
Mike Saunders/Jillian Burgess
Charlotte Styles

CONTENTS

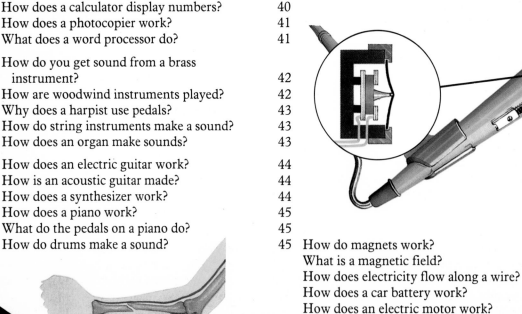

TRANSPORTATION

OUT IN SPACE

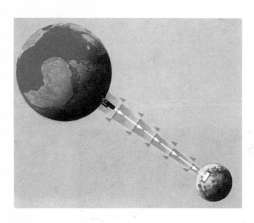

PLANET EARTH

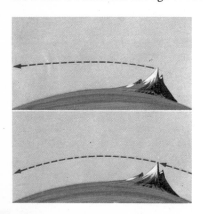

PLANTS AND ANIMALS

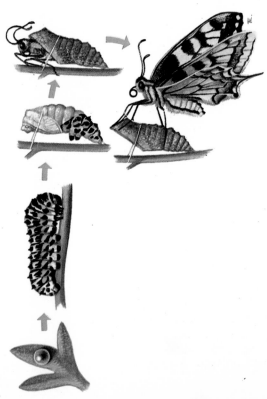

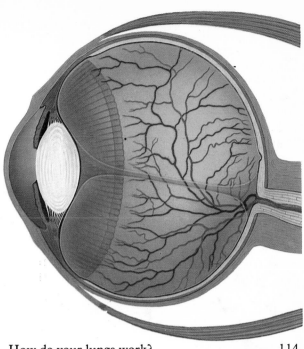

OURSELVES

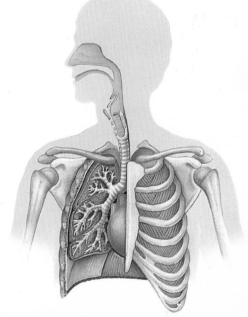

SCIENCE AND TECHNOLOGY

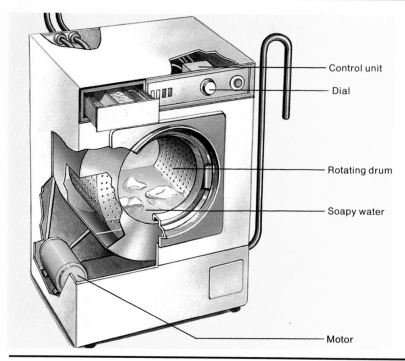

Control unit

Dial

Rotating drum

Soapy water

Motor

◀ HOW DOES A WASHING MACHINE WORK?

Most washing machines have a round drum that spins to wash the clothes. The clothes tumble over each other as it turns, which helps the washing powder to clean them. The clothes are then rinsed in clean water to remove the dirty, soapy water.

The clothes may be washed and rinsed several times in the washing machine to get them really clean. Then they are spun very quickly to remove most of the water so that they will dry quickly.

▶ HOW DOES A REFRIGERATOR WORK?

In the sides of a refrigerator are pipes that contain a cold fluid. This makes the inside of the refrigerator cold. The cold fluid is pumped through the pipes to carry heat away from the food in the refrigerator and keep it cold.

The fluid that circulates in the pipes of the refrigerator easily changes from a liquid to a vapor. As it enters the interior, it is liquid and is pumped through an evaporator. This lowers its pressure and it becomes vapor. The change from liquid to vapor makes the vapor cold because it takes up heat. The cold vapor then flows

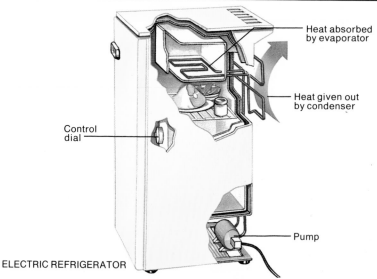

Heat absorbed by evaporator

Heat given out by condenser

Control dial

Pump

ELECTRIC REFRIGERATOR

through pipes inside the refrigerator.

After it leaves, it goes to a condenser, which increases its pressure so that it changes back into a liquid. As this happens, the fluid gives out heat. You can feel this heat coming from the warm pipes at the back of the refrigerator. In this way, heat is taken from the interior of the refrigerator to the outside, where it disperses. Either electricity or gas may be used to power refrigerators.

► HOW DOES A DISHWASHER WORK?

You load the dirty dishes and cutlery into the dishwasher. It first sprays the dishes with hot water to wash away all the grease and dirt. Then it heats the dishes and cutlery to dry it.

A dishwashing machine has a control dial to set a program of washing and rinsing. This depends on the kind of dishes and cutlery being washed and on how dirty they are. First, the machine's heater warms the washing water to about 158°F, much hotter than the hands can bear. Then spinning bars spray jets of hot water over the utensils to clean them.

The water may contain detergents to dissolve grease and wetting agents to help rinse away the dirt. The dishwasher's control unit adds these substances to the water when they are needed, and times the washing program. Finally, the dishwasher's heater may be used to dry the utensils.

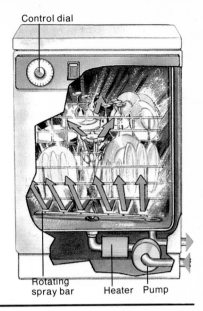

Control dial

Rotating spray bar   Heater   Pump

◄ HOW DO SCALES WORK?

The scales used to weigh food in the kitchen are called spring balances. When the pan is loaded, it squeezes a spring inside the balance. This makes a pointer turn and shows the weight. When the food is taken off the pan, the spring pushes or pulls the pointer back again.

Bathroom scales work in the same way as kitchen scales. They have a much stronger spring because they weigh people, who may be heavy.

Inside the scales, a rack and pinion gear is connected to the pointer or dial. As the pan is pushed down, it moves the gear and the pointer or dial turns to indicate the weight. The pan rests on a spring so that the distance it moves depends on the weight pushing it down.

Electronic scales have a device that produces an electric signal when they are loaded. This signal goes to a small computer that calculates the weight and lights up the display on the scales.

Pointer

Dial   Rack and pinion gear   Spring

► HOW DOES A MICROWAVE OVEN WORK?

A microwave oven does not have burning flames or red-hot plates like gas and electric ovens. You put the food into a metal box and press a switch. Inside the box, invisible heat rays bombard the food and cook it very quickly.

A microwave oven gets its name from the rays that cook the food, which are called microwaves. They are like radio waves, and the rays heat up objects in the same way as the Sun's rays warm us. However, microwaves penetrate into the food, so that it cooks on the inside as well as outside. In an ordinary oven, it takes time for the heat to get to the inside of the food. Microwaves heat up the inside immediately, which is why a microwave oven cooks or heats up food so quickly.

Some microwave ovens contain small computers that automatically cook the food at the correct temperature for the right length of time.

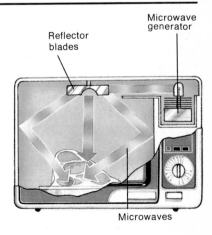

Reflector blades

Microwave generator

Microwaves

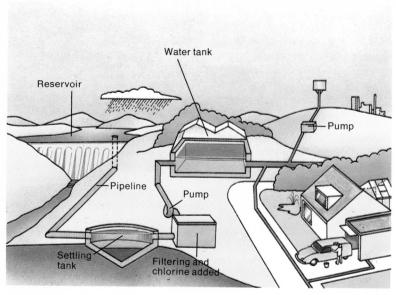

Reservoir · Water tank · Pump · Pipeline · Pump · Settling tank · Filtering and chlorine added

▲ HOW DOES WATER GET TO THE HOME?

Water comes to a house through underground pipes. It usually comes from a large reservoir fed by a river or stream. Then it may go to a big tank on high ground above the homes in a region so that the water then flows down to the houses there.

Reservoirs are formed by building dams across river valleys so that huge lakes of water pile up behind them.

Water also comes directly from lakes and rivers or from wells dug deep in the ground. In all cases, the water is rainwater. It either falls on high ground and then flows into rivers and lakes, or it soaks away underground and fills wells.

From the reservoirs, lakes, rivers or wells, the water goes to water works to be purified. The pure water is then pumped to water tanks or water towers to be stored. Then it flows through pipes to homes by gravity, or it is pumped to houses.

◄ HOW IS WATER MADE SAFE FOR DRINKING?

The water we take from reservoirs, lakes, rivers and wells is not always fit to drink. Before it reaches homes, it goes to water works to be purified. There chemicals are added to kill germs and to remove dirt from the water. The water also goes through filters to make it clean.

The first stage in purifying water is to remove particles of dirt and bacteria. This is done by adding chemicals that make them clump together and settle on the bottom of the purification tanks. The water is filtered again by passing it through beds of sand to trap any dirt particles and bacteria that remain. Then the water may be treated to kill any disease germs, for example, by adding chlorine.

Other chemicals may be added to improve the water. Fluoride is sometimes added to water to help strengthen teeth. Water softeners stop the water from producing a deposit that clogs up pipes.

► HOW DOES SOAP CLEAN THINGS?

Things get dirty because particles of dust and dirt stick to them. Soapy water dissolves the grease that makes dust and dirt stick to the clothes. The particles float away into the water, and the things are cleaned.

Ordinary water does not remove dirt from things because grease and water do not mix. Soap is made of long thin molecules that attach

themselves to water molecules at one end and to grease molecules at the other end. In this way, the soap molecules link the water and grease molecules so that the grease dissolves and is washed away with the water.

Detergents like liquid soap work in exactly the same way as regular soap.

Soap is made by boiling caustic soda with animal fats such as tallow, and vegetable oils such as coconut oil. Most soap is also perfumed and colored. Detergents are made from petroleum

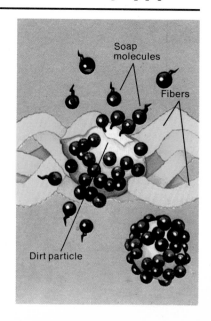

Soap molecules · Fibers · Dirt particle

▶ HOW DO DRAINS AND SEWERS WORK?

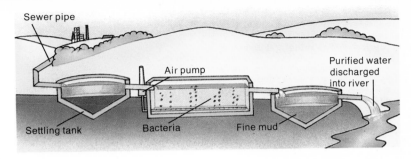

Drains and sewers carry waste water away from homes. Rainwater drains carry rainwater to soak away in the ground. Waste water from kitchens, bathrooms and toilets goes through pipes under the ground to be purified.

Houses in the country often have a septic tank. This is a large underground tank in the garden into which waste water is piped. The water is purified inside the tank and soaks away in the ground.

In cities and towns, waste water goes into sewer pipes under the streets. These pipes take the waste to sewage disposal plants, where the waste water goes through settling tanks and filters to remove solid wastes.

The water may also be treated in tanks with air and bacteria that consume the impurities in the water. The water is then clean enough to be piped to a river or the sea.

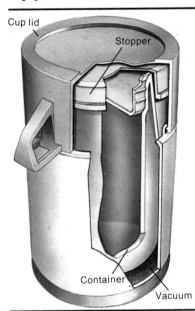

◀ HOW DOES A THERMOS KEEP THINGS HOT?

A thermos bottle can keep drinks hot for several hours. This is because the thermos stops as much heat escaping from the drink as possible. As the drink loses very little heat, it keeps hot for a long time.

A thermos is designed to prevent heat loss in several ways. The silver walls of the container inside the thermos reflect heat rays back into the container. In addition, there is a vacuum between the walls of the container to stop heat flowing through the walls. The container is surrounded by an outer shell made of insulating materials that slow down the rate of heat loss. In this way, heat leaks out of the thermos very slowly.

A thermos is not only used for keeping things hot. Because heat does not flow out of the thermos quickly, it does not easily enter the thermos either. For this reason, things like iced drinks or liquid air can be kept cold in a thermos bottle.

▶ HOW DOES A PRESSURE COOKER WORK?

A pressure cooker is like a large saucepan with a tight-fitting lid. A little water is put in the cooker with the food. When the cooker is heated, the water boils and produces steam inside the cooker. This steam makes the food cook very quickly.

The reason that food cooks quickly inside a pressure cooker is that it gets very hot. When the water boils inside the cooker, the steam that is produced cannot get out. It builds up a high pressure inside the cooker.

Steam that is at a high pressure is hotter than ordinary steam that comes out of a kettle. The greater the pressure, the hotter the steam and the faster the food cooks. On the lid of the cooker is a valve that lets some steam out when the pressure reaches a certain level. The valve can be set to raise or lower the steam pressure inside the cooker. In this way, the temperature can be changed.

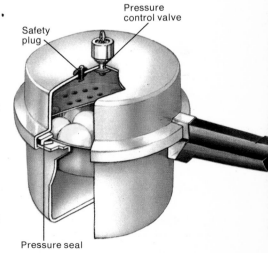

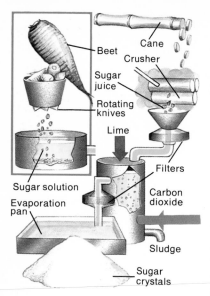

Beet
Cane
Crusher
Sugar juice
Rotating knives
Lime
Sugar solution
Evaporation pan
Filters
Carbon dioxide
Sludge
Sugar crystals

◄ HOW IS SUGAR MADE?

Most sugar comes from two plants: sugar cane and sugar beet. To make sugar, the cane or beet is crushed or cut and treated with water. The water dissolves the sugar in the plants. Then the water is heated to produce sugar crystals.

Sugar cane comes from tropical countries and is a tall grass plant like bamboo. The sugar is in the stalks of the cane. Sugar beet grows in cooler regions and is a root crop like carrots. The sugar is in the root of the beet.

In sugar mills, the stalks of sugar cane are crushed to obtain sugar juice, which is then washed into pans. Sugar beet is sliced and then soaked in hot water to extract the sugar juice. The solution of sugar juice extracted from the cane or beet is then filtered and heated to make the sugar crystallize. This raw sugar is light brown. To make white sugar, the raw sugar is dissolved in water and the solution is then filtered and heated to crystallize again.

► WHERE DOES SALT COME FROM?

Salt is a mineral, found in the sea and under the ground. To get salt, sea water is let into shallow pools at the shore. There the Sun's heat makes the water evaporate, leaving the salt behind. Salt is also mined underground.

The salt that is obtained from the sea and mined underground is not totally pure. To make the table salt that we use in cooking, it is purified. The

impure salt is dissolved in hot water, and the brine (salt solution) goes to evaporators. These reduce the air pressure to make the brine boil, and pure crystals of salt form in the brine.

Salt is also obtained from salt wells, which are pipes drilled down into salt deposits. Water is forced down the pipes to dissolve the salt, and the brine produced is pumped to the surface.

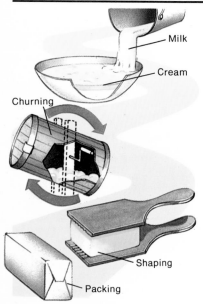

Milk
Cream
Churning
Shaping
Packing

◄ HOW IS BUTTER MADE?

Butter comes from the cream in cow's milk. The cream is skimmed from the milk and then placed in a spinning drum to churn it. This turns the cream into butter. Before the butter is packed, salt may be added to flavor it. The butter may also be colored to make it golden.

Cream is made up of drops of liquid fat floating in the milk. To separate the cream, the milk is whirled in a centrifuge. The cream is then heated to pasteurize it (kill germs) to stop it going sour or rancid. Then the cream is churned in a revolving drum with baffles. This forces the drops of fat to come together, producing butter. The liquid left over is called buttermilk.

The butter is then salted and colored if necessary, and finally cut up into blocks and packed. Butter is also made without salt, and some butter has a pleasing natural color and does not need to be colored.

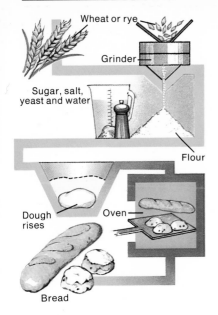

▲ WHAT IS BREAD MADE OF?

Bread is made from wheat or rye, which is ground into flour. Then the flour is mixed with yeast, water, sugar and salt to make dough. The dough is cut into blocks which are then baked in an oven to make loaves of bread.

Dough is made by mixing flour, yeast, water, sugar and salt and then allowing this mixture to ferment. The yeast causes the dough to rise by forming bubbles of carbon dioxide gas in the dough.

The dough is then formed into the shape of a loaf and baked in a loaf tin in the oven. The heat causes the dough to rise some more, making the bread light. Then the heat kills the yeast so that the bread sets in a loaf shape. The crust forms and the bread is cooked.

After the loaf has cooled, the baker may slice and wrap it. Bread is white or brown depending on whether white or brown flour is used.

▼ HOW DO BUBBLES GET INTO FIZZY DRINKS?

When you open a fizzy drink, bubbles form inside the drink. These are bubbles of a gas called carbon dioxide, and help to make the drink taste sharp. The gas is dissolved in the drink when it is made at the factory.

At the factory, carbon dioxide gas is forced into the drink under pressure so that it dissolves in the liquid. The drink remains under pressure in the bottle or can so that the gas stays dissolved in the drink. However, when the bottle or can is opened, the pressure is released. This is why the drink hisses as it is opened. The carbon dioxide escapes and forms bubbles.

You can also make fizzy drinks by adding water to drink powders. As well as flavors, the powders contain chemicals such as sodium bicarbonate and citric acid that make carbon dioxide when added to water. The gas produces bubbles in the water as it is formed.

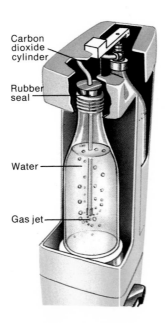

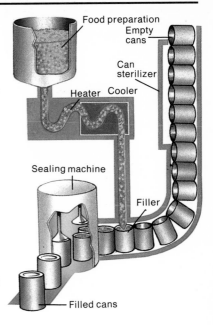

▲ HOW IS FOOD PACKED IN CANS?

Food that is packed in cans stays fresh because air and germs are removed from inside the cans. A can has no lid when it is filled with food. Air and germs are removed, and the lid is sealed to make it airtight. This is done in a canning factory.

The food that is stored in cans has to be made sterile and free from germs to keep it fresh. Air also has to be kept away from the food because it would bring germs to it.

In a canning factory, the food is prepared in large containers. It is cooked if necessary and then goes to the canning machine, which is fed with a line of empty cans. The food is placed in the cans, with a liquid such as sauce or syrup. Air is removed and the lids are sealed onto the cans. The cans are then heated to sterilize the food inside.

With some foods, the cans and food are sterilized first by heating before the cans are filled.

15

▶ HOW DO LOCKS WORK?

When a door is locked, a bolt or bar moves out of the lock and fits into a slot in the door frame. Unlocking the door slides the bolt back. When the key is put into the lock, it frees the bolt so that it can move. Turning the key then moves the bolt.

In a cylinder lock such as a Yale lock, the center of the lock turns. The key raises a set of pins that normally hold the center fixed to the rest of

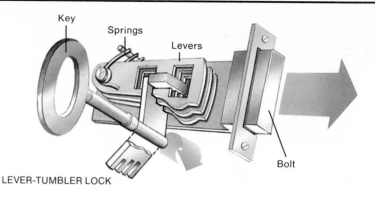

Key
Springs
Levers
Bolt

LEVER-TUMBLER LOCK

the lock so that it cannot move.

A lever-tumbler lock contains a set of levers that hold the bolt closed or open. Springs keep the levers in

position so that the bolt cannot move. When the key is turned, the levers are raised and line up to free the bolt. The key moves the bolt in or out to lock or open the door.

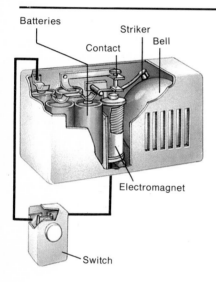

Batteries
Striker
Contact
Bell
Electromagnet
Switch

◀ HOW DOES A DOORBELL WORK?

When you push a button to ring a doorbell, an electric current goes to the bell. The current powers a magnet in the bell, and the magnet moves a striker to hit the bell and make it ring. Some doorbells are not electric, but work by clockwork instead.

In an electric doorbell, the button is a switch that connects a supply of electricity to the bell. The

current goes through a contact to an electromagnet. This produces a magnetic field that moves the striker, which hits the bell. As it does so, the contact passing the current to the electromagnet opens. The current ceases to flow to the electromagnet, and a spring pulls the striker back. The contact then closes and current passes again to the electromagnet. The bell rings again and opens the contact again.

In this way, the bell keeps on ringing as long as the button is pressed.

▶ HOW DOES A CLOCK WORK?

In clocks that you wind up, a spring or a weight makes the hands go round. Gears turn the minute hand 12 times as fast as the hour hand. A pendulum or another device keeps the hands turning at the correct speed so that the clock is right. In electric clocks, an electric motor turns the hands.

Inside a pendulum clock is a toothed wheel called an

escape wheel. This wheel is driven around by a spring that is wound tight, or by a drum that has a cord and a weight attached to it. The weight turns the drum as it falls. The escape wheel is controlled by an anchor that rocks to and fro. The anchor is connected to a pendulum that swings at a constant rate, and the ends of the anchor allow the teeth of the escape wheel to pass as the pendulum swings.

In this way, the escape wheel turns at a constant rate and the hands are connected by gears to the escape wheel.

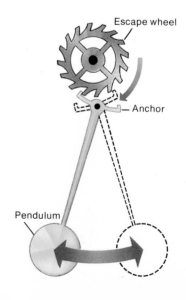

Escape wheel
Anchor
Pendulum

► HOW DOES AN IRON WORK?

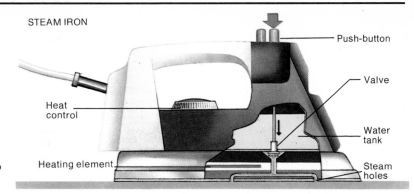

STEAM IRON

Push-button

Valve

Heat control

Water tank

Heating element

Steam holes

A hot iron smooths out creases in cloth. Most irons are powered by electricity. Inside the iron is an electric heater. A steam iron makes steam to make the cloth slightly damp. This helps to remove creases and wrinkles that a dry iron could not manage.

An electric iron has a heat control that sends more current to the heating element to make it hotter. A steam iron contains a water tank in which water is boiled by the heating element to make steam. A push-button on top of the iron opens a valve to let the steam through holes in the base. With the button up, no steam gets through to the cloth and the iron works like an ordinary iron.

◄ HOW DOES AN AEROSOL SPRAY WORK?

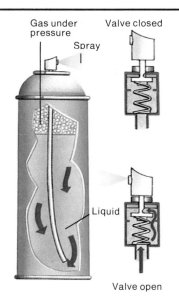

Gas under pressure

Valve closed

Spray

Liquid

Valve open

When you press down the nozzle of an aerosol can, a spray comes from the hole in the top. The spray is made of fine drops of liquid. Inside the can, a gas under pressure forces the liquid up a tube to the top. When the top is pressed, the hole opens and the liquid sprays out.

The gas that is under pressure inside the can is called a propellant because it propels the liquid up the tube and out of the hole in the top. It consists of a gas that is harmless and does not dissolve in the liquid inside the can. The top of the can contains a valve with a spring that closes the valve when the top is released.

Aerosol cans are used to spray paints, deodorants, furniture polish, oven cleaner, pesticides and many other liquid products.

Because an aerosol can contains a gas under pressure, it is dangerous to heat the can as it may explode.

► HOW DOES A VACUUM CLEANER WORK?

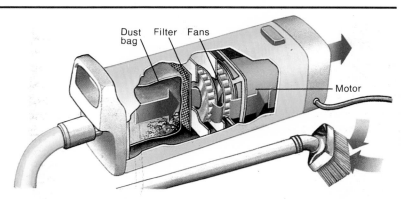

Dust bag   Filter   Fans

Motor

A vacuum cleaner sucks in air at one end, and as it does so, it sucks up dust and dirt. The dust and dirt are trapped in a bag inside the cleaner. The cleaner contains an electric motor which drives fans that suck in the air.

The vacuum cleaner may have brushes that stir up dust and dirt on the floor or in the carpet so that the cleaner can suck them in.

In some cleaners, the brushes are driven round by the motor. Inside the cleaner, a partial vacuum is created as the fans blow air out of the cleaner. Air rushes in to fill the vacuum, bringing dust and dirt with it. To avoid damage to the fans and motor, a filter traps anything that might get sucked into the cleaner.

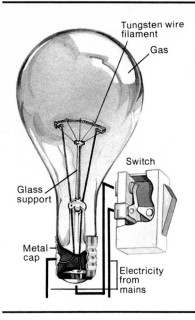

Tungsten wire filament

Gas

Switch

Glass support

Metal cap

Electricity from mains

◀ HOW DOES AN ELECTRIC LIGHT WORK?

When you switch on the light, electricity goes through the switch to the light bulb. In the bulb is a thin wire called a filament. When electricity reaches the filament, it makes it hot, so hot that it glows with light.

The filament in a light bulb is made of tungsten. This metal has a very high melting point, so the filament does not melt when it gets white-hot. The bulb also contains a gas such as argon that does not combine with tungsten. If the bulb contained air, the oxygen would combine with the tungsten and the bulb would immediately burn out.

The filament glows because it resists the flow of electricity. The greater its resistance, the hotter it gets and the brighter it glows. A bright bulb uses more electricity than a less bright bulb. The brightness of a light bulb is measured in watts. A medium-sized room needs a 100-watt bulb.

▶ HOW DOES A FLASH-LIGHT WORK?

When you switch on a flashlight, electricity flows from the batteries inside the flashlight to the bulb, which lights up. Behind the bulb, a curved mirror reflects the light from the bulb.

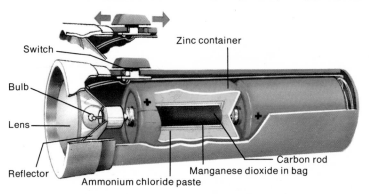

Switch

Zinc container

Bulb

Lens

Reflector

Ammonium chloride paste

Manganese dioxide in bag

Carbon rod

The bulb in a flashlight is like an electric light bulb, except that it lights up with a low current from a few volts. This current is supplied by batteries. The batteries contain chemicals that produce an electric current when the flashlight is switched on. They are connected through the switch to the bulb.

The reflector behind the bulb and the lens in front make the light form a beam. When the beam lights up an object, an image of the glowing bulb falls on it.

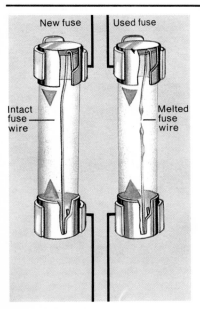

New fuse

Used fuse

Intact fuse wire

Melted fuse wire

◀ HOW DO FUSES AND CIRCUIT BREAKERS WORK?

All electrical systems have fuses or circuit breakers of some kind. If too much electricity flows through an electric wire, it can start a fire. Fuses and circuit breakers are put into electrical circuits to stop this happening. They cut off the electricity before any damage is done.

Fuses and circuit breakers work in different ways, but they are both designed to break electrical circuits before fires or explosions can occur. Fuses normally contain a thin wire made of a metal that melts at a low temperature. If too much current passes through the fuse wire, it heats up and melts, breaking the circuit.

In circuit breakers, an overload of current usually operates an electromagnet which trips the contact mechanism and breaks the circuit.

The usual cause of too much current is a short circuit.

▶ HOW DOES THE TELEPHONE WORK?

When you speak to someone on the telephone, an electric signal goes from the mouthpiece. It travels along wires to the other telephone. There it works the earpiece so that the other person hears you. The other person talks back to you in the same way.

The mouthpiece of a telephone contains a small microphone. The sound waves from your voice make a diaphragm vibrate and this compresses carbon granules in the microphone. An electric current flows through the microphone, and the granules vary its strength as you speak.

This varying current then flows along wires to the telephone exchange, which sends it on to the other telephone. There it enters a small loudspeaker in the earpiece. This contains an electromagnet which causes a diaphragm to vibrate as the incoming current varies. This produces the sound of your voice.

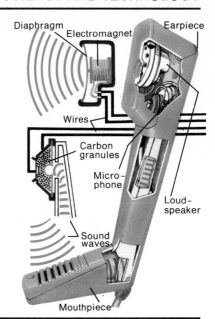

Diaphragm · Electromagnet · Earpiece · Wires · Carbon granules · Microphone · Loudspeaker · Sound waves · Mouthpiece

◀ HOW CAN ROOMS BE MADE SOUNDPROOF?

Sound travels through the glass panes of windows. It is soaked up by cloth, so drawing heavy curtains over a window helps to keep out sound. Having two window panes, as in double-glazing, can also prevent sound getting through.

Sound waves travel through air and even through hard materials such as glass, stone and brick. However, the waves get weaker as they travel, and not much sound gets through thick walls. A glass window pane is too thin to keep out sound, but two panes placed at least eight inches apart weaken the sound waves so that they do not penetrate.

Soft materials such as cloth absorb sound waves. To make rooms such as recording studios totally soundproof, the walls have no windows. The walls and ceiling are also lined with sound-absorbing materials like cork and plastic foam.

▶ HOW DOES A HEATING SYSTEM WORK?

Central heating is a way of heating a house or building. Each room has a heater that is supplied with heat from a boiler or another source of heat. The heaters automatically warm the rooms to the right temperature. They switch themselves on and off when necessary.

In many heating systems, hot water from a central boiler flows through radiators. The boiler may use gas, coal or oil as a fuel to heat the water. The system also heats the water that comes from the hot taps. A pump circulates the hot water around the system.

Instead of a hot water system, many homes and buildings are heated by warm air. Fans blow the air from a central heater through pipes to the rooms. Electric heating systems have radiators powered by electricity, or electric heating elements in the floors or ceilings.

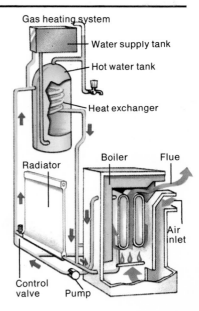

Gas heating system · Water supply tank · Hot water tank · Heat exchanger · Radiator · Boiler · Flue · Air inlet · Control valve · Pump

▶ HOW DOES A LIGHTNING ROD WORK?

When lightning strikes, a giant electric spark travels between the clouds and the ground. A lightning rod is a long strip of metal that runs from the top of a building to the bottom. It carries the electricity in the lightning safely to the ground.

During a thunderstorm, a huge electric charge builds up in the clouds. This causes another electric charge to build up on the ground. If the charges get too big, electricity flows between them and a flash of lightning occurs.

Lightning strikes high buildings, so lightning rods are fixed to them to prevent damage. The electric charge builds up more at the tip of the rod, which is pointed. If lightning is about to strike, it is likely to hit the lightning rod first. The rod carries the electricity that flows between the ground and the clouds, so that no damage is done to the building.

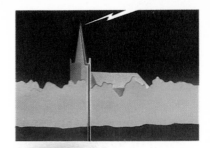

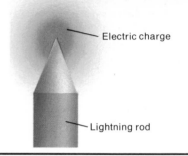

Electric charge

Lightning rod

◀ HOW DOES A GREENHOUSE STAY WARM?

It is warmer inside a greenhouse than it is outside. This is why gardeners use them to grow plants. Heat rays from the sky enter the greenhouse through the glass windows. The heat rays cannot escape and warm the greenhouse.

The heat rays that enter the greenhouse come from the Sun, even if it is cloudy. They warm the inside of the greenhouse, just as they warm the ground. But outside, the ground produces its own heat rays which go back to the sky, so the ground does not get very warm.

However, inside the greenhouse the heat rays from the plants and floor are stopped by the glass. They cannot get out, and so the inside of the greenhouse gets warmer than it does outside. This happens because the heat rays from the Sun and those from the plants are different. This is because the Sun is very hot and the plants are not.

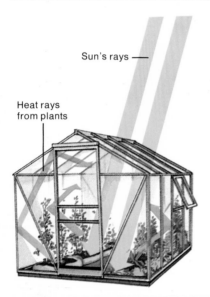

Sun's rays

Heat rays from plants

▶ WHAT DOES AN ANTENNA DO?

To make a television or radio set work, it has to have an antenna. The antenna picks up the television or radio signals that come through the air. In the antenna, these signals change into tiny electric currents. Inside the set, these currents are turned into pictures and sound.

Television and radio signals are invisible rays that come from transmitters. When the rays meet a metal object, they produce very low electric signals. An antenna is designed to pick up as weak a signal as possible, so it may have to be pointed towards the transmitter. If the transmitter is far away, a large antenna may be needed. For radio, a single metal rod, sometimes inside the set, is usually enough to get a good signal. Television sets need a stronger signal, so many television antennas have several bars of metal which increase the strength of the signal detected.

▼ HOW DO STREET LIGHTS WORK?

Most street lights work by electricity. Some lights have bulbs like the light bulbs in our houses. Mirrors behind the bulbs reflect light down into the street. Bright street lights have tubes of gases that glow when electricity flows through them.

The street lights that glow bright orange are called sodium vapor lamps. They consist of tubes containing the metal sodium and a gas called neon. When an electric current passes through the tube, it makes the neon glow red. The tube warms up and the sodium vaporizes. As the sodium vapor mixes with the neon, it glows orange. The light is very bright, and the tubes use little electricity.

The white lights in city streets are mercury vapor lamps, which contain mercury instead of sodium. The mercury vapor produces invisible ultraviolet light. The inner coating of the tube contains substances that glow brightly in ultraviolet light.

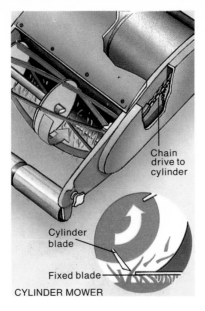

Chain drive to cylinder

Cylinder blade

Fixed blade

CYLINDER MOWER

▲ HOW DOES A LAWNMOWER WORK?

A lawnmower has sharp blades to cut grass. A cylinder mower has blades arranged in a cylinder shape. These turn to sweep the grass against a fixed blade. A rotary mower has blades that spin and cut the grass directly. Mowers may be powered by gasoline engines or electricity.

The cylinder blades and fixed blade on a cylinder mower cut the grass like scissors. The cylinder is driven around by the wheels and in some machines the wheels also act as rollers that flatten the grass. A grass bag may be fixed to the mower to catch the cuttings. Cylinder mowers can be pushed or they may be powered by small gasoline engines or electricity. In very large mowers, the gardener rides on the mower.

Rotary mowers have a set of horizontal blades that are driven by an electric motor or gasoline engine. Some rotary machines produce a cushion of air so that they float above the grass as they cut it.

▼ HOW DO TRAFFIC LIGHTS WORK?

Traffic lights contain electric light bulbs with red, yellow and green glass in front. The lights are operated by control units with timers or computers. Detectors in the road tell the computers how many vehicles are approaching the lights. The computers change the lights.

Some traffic lights change at set times. These may be temporary lights placed to direct traffic around an obstacle. In some cities, sets of timed lights are linked together so that traffic can travel along a main road at a certain speed without stopping.

Many traffic lights are controlled by computers linked to detectors in the road as well as to a central traffic control computer. The detectors contain electric circuits in which the metal vehicle produces a signal as it passes. The central computer can operate sets of lights to allow the traffic to flow easily.

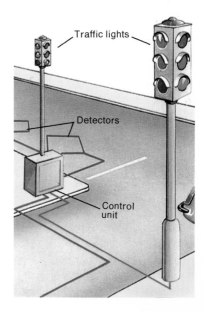

Traffic lights

Detectors

Control unit

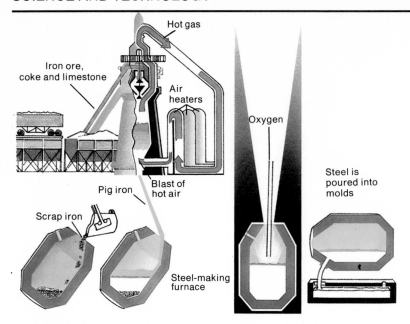

Hot gas

Iron ore, coke and limestone

Air heaters

Oxygen

Steel is poured into molds

Pig iron

Blast of hot air

Scrap iron

Steel-making furnace

▲ WHAT IS STEEL MADE FOR?

Steel is the most important metal. It is used to make many things, from huge constructions like bridges, ships and frameworks for buildings down to tiny objects such as pins and needles. Most metal things we use are made of steel.

Steel is used so much because it is cheap and also because it is hard and strong. It is cheap because it is made from iron, which is a very common metal. Pure iron is not much used, because it is not very hard. Steel is made by adding carbon to iron.

Metals are added to steel to make it suitable for many uses. These metals can make steel very hard so that it does not wear out quickly when it is used. This steel is very useful for moving parts in machines, such as gears. The steel can also be made very elastic for use in springs, and it can be made resistant to heat and rust for tanks and pipes.

◄ HOW IS STEEL MADE?

Steel is made from iron ore, a mineral dug from the ground. The ore is mixed with coke and lime-stone and the mixture is heated in a big tower called a blast furnace. This makes pig iron. The pig iron is then treated with oxygen gas to make steel.

When iron ore is heated with coke and limestone in a blast furnace, a mixture of iron and carbon called pig iron is produced. The carbon comes from the coke. The limestone takes up other materials that are not wanted. A blast of hot air is driven through the iron ore mixture as it descends in the blast furnace. Molten pig iron is formed at the base of the furnace. Hot gases from the top of the furnace heat the air that is fed to the furnace.

The pig iron has too much carbon to make steel, so the extra carbon is burned off by blowing oxygen over it. Scrap iron may be added first. The molten steel produced is then poured into moulds to make steel blocks.

▶ HOW DOES WELDING WORK?

Welding is a way of joining two pieces of metal. The welder has a tool that heats the metal where the pieces are joined. On the surface of each piece, the metal melts and flows together. Then it sets to give a strong joint.

A welding torch may be used to weld metals together. It burns gases such as acetylene or hydrogen to give a hot flame. The torch also has a

supply of oxygen to make the flame very hot, and it can even be used underwater.

Welders also use electricity to join metals. An electric current is passed through the metals at the place they are to be joined. The powerful current melts the metals at the point of contact and joins them together. As the welder joins the metals, he may use a rod of metal. This melts to build up the joint and a flux strengthens the joint. The bright light can damage the eyes, so welders wear dark goggles or masks.

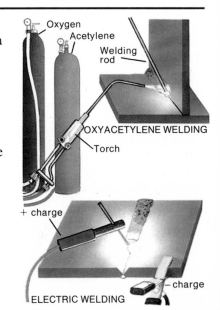

Oxygen

Acetylene

Welding rod

OXYACETYLENE WELDING

Torch

+ charge

− charge

ELECTRIC WELDING

▶ HOW IS GLASS MADE?

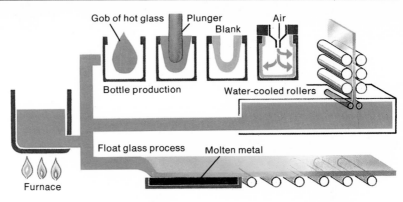

Gob of hot glass · Plunger · Air
Blank
Bottle production · Water-cooled rollers
Float glass process · Molten metal
Furnace

Glass is made from sand, lime and soda. These are heated in a furnace and they all melt together to produce molten glass. Before it sets hard, the hot glass is soft and it can be made into any shape. Other ingredients may be added to make the glass stronger or to color it.

The sand used to make glass has to be very pure, and it comes from sandstone that is dug out of the ground in quarries. Soda is made from salt, and lime comes from rocks such as limestone. Glass made from these three materials is used for bottles, windows, light bulbs and many other common glass objects. A strong glass suitable for cooking dishes is made with borax, and lead and potash are added to the glass used to make lenses.

◀ HOW IS GLASS COLORED AND SHAPED?

Colored glass is made by adding certain metals to the ingredients. Glass blowers form gobs of hot glass into shapes such as a vase. They blow down a tube into the hot glass to make it bulge into shape.

The green color of bottles is produced by iron in the sand used to make glass. Other metals give different colors. For example, cobalt gives deep blue glass and copper makes glass bright red.

Sheet or plate glass for windows is made by drawing the molten glass from the furnace through rollers. The rollers cool the glass so that it becomes soft and squeeze it into a flat sheet. The sheet is then treated to make it strong and polished to make it smooth.

The float glass process produces smooth plate glass by floating the molten glass on top of a bath of molten metal. The metal is less hot than the glass, which sets to form a solid sheet.

▶ HOW IS RUBBER MADE?

Some rubber comes from rubber trees, which grow in hot, tropical regions of the world. The bark of the tree is cut to give a fluid called latex that contains the rubber. The rubber is then made into different shapes. Most rubber nowadays is made from chemicals in factories and no longer comes from rubber trees.

Rubber trees are tapped, or cut, to produce latex, a milky

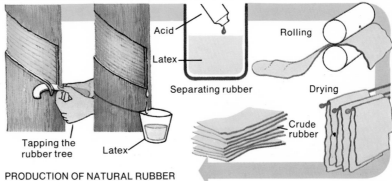

Acid · Rolling
Latex
Separating rubber · Drying
Crude rubber
Tapping the rubber tree · Latex

PRODUCTION OF NATURAL RUBBER

sap, which is then treated to give crude rubber. Crude rubber can also be made artificially from chemicals.

The crude rubber is then mixed with coloring materials and chemicals that make the rubber strong and long-lasting. Then it is placed in machines that shape it into a variety of products, such as car tires and hoses.

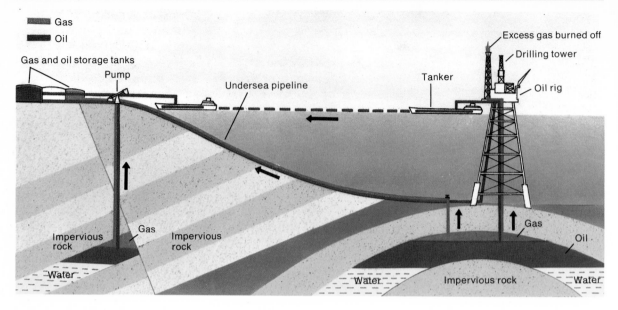

Gas
Oil
Gas and oil storage tanks
Pump
Undersea pipeline
Tanker
Excess gas burned off
Drilling tower
Oil rig
Impervious rock
Gas
Impervious rock
Water
Water
Impervious rock
Gas
Oil
Water

▲ WHERE DOES NATURAL GAS COME FROM?

Natural gas comes from under the ground and under the sea. Holes are drilled to get the gas. Then it flows through pipes to homes for use in cookers and heaters. Natural gas is also used in factories to make products like fuel and plastics.

Natural gas forms in deposits deep underground. It is made of the remains of creatures and plants that were buried long ago. The gas is trapped in layers of rock, often together with oil. It is obtained in the same way as oil, and then piped to homes and factories.

Natural gas consists mainly of methane, which has no smell. Small amounts of strong-smelling substances are added to gas which is to be used as a fuel so that a leak can quickly be detected.

The methane in natural gas is also used to make chemicals for industry, such as methyl alcohol, and fuels such as butane. It is also a source of the light gas helium.

▲ HOW IS OIL OBTAINED?

Large deposits of oil lie beneath the sea or under the ground. They are found with instruments that detect the rocks underground. To get the oil, holes are drilled down to the deposits and lined with pipes. Oil may flow up a pipe by itself, or it may be pumped up.

Oil is found by seismic surveying. Scientists explode a small charge on the surface. A shock wave travels into the ground and bounces back off the rocks. The waves that come back give the scientists a picture of the rocks beneath. Oil is often trapped under a dome of impervious rock, beneath a cap of natural gas.

Oilmen then drill down to the oil, using a drilling bit that bites into the rock. They feed pipes into the hole to line it. The oil flows up the drill pipe, and into a pipeline that takes it to storage tanks. At first, it is forced up by the pressure of gas or water around it. Later, it may have to be pumped up.

▲ HOW DOES AN OIL RIG WORK?

An oil rig has a high drilling tower. From this, a long shaft with a drill at the end digs down into the ground. Oil rigs at sea drill into the sea bed from the surface.

Most oil drills have a bit made of rotating teeth that chew through the rock. The bit is placed at the end of a shaft that revolves and turns the bit. New lengths of shaft are added as the bit drills deeper. An outer steel casing is also fed into the hole as it is drilled to prevent it from collapsing.

When oil is struck, the drill pipe is connected to a pipeline to take the oil to storage tanks. When oil is being drilled at sea, the oil rig may have legs that stand on the sea bed. If the sea is too deep, the rig floats at the surface and is anchored in position.

When oil has been found, it may go directly from the sea floor into a pipeline or it may be taken ashore from the rig by tankers.

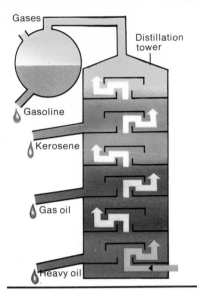

Gases
Distillation tower
Gasoline
Kerosene
Gas oil
Heavy oil

◀ HOW IS GASOLINE MANUFACTURED?

Gasoline comes from the oil that is drilled from under the ground or under the sea. The gasoline is distilled in a refinery. The oil is heated and goes to a tower. The gasoline vaporizes and the vapor leaves the top of the tower. It is then cooled to give gas.

Gasoline is not the only product distilled from oil. It also produces kerosene and lubricating oils. These products vaporize with the gasoline, but they have higher boiling points. The vapors get cooler as they rise and condense at different levels, from which they are piped off.

Another refining process called "cracking" is carried out on the heavy oils left behind. They are heated under pressure so that they break down into gasoline and gases such as ethylene, that go to make plastics. However, these gases may also be converted into gasoline by a process known as reforming.

▶ HOW ARE PLASTICS MADE?

Plastics are made from chemicals that come from coal and oil. When the chemicals are heated they combine together to make plastics. The plastics are then made into shapes. Some chemicals make soft plastics and others make hard plastics.

The chemicals used to make plastics have small molecules. When plastics form, the molecules join together in long chains to make large molecules. For example, molecules of the gas ethylene join to form long-chain molecules of polyethylene, which is a plastic. Substances with long-chain molecules are called polymers, which is why many plastics have names beginning with poly-.

When some plastics are made, they set hard and stay rigid. They have to be molded into shape as they are made. These are thermosetting plastics. Other plastics soften when they are warmed. These thermoplastic plastics can be heated to shape them.

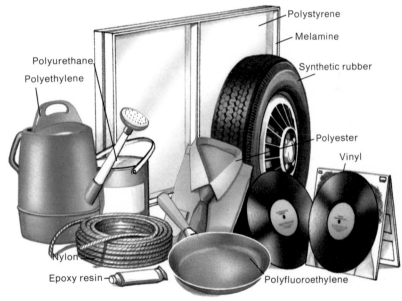

Polyurethane
Polyethylene
Polystyrene
Melamine
Synthetic rubber
Polyester
Vinyl
Nylon
Epoxy resin
Polyfluoroethylene

▲ HOW ARE PLASTICS USED?

Plastics have very many uses because there are many different kinds. They can be soft or hard, rigid or flexible, clear or colored. Plastics are therefore used to make all sorts of containers and structures. Plastics can also be made into thread, cloth, paints and glues.

In thermoplastic plastics, the long-chain molecules can bend. This makes the plastic soft or flexible. These plastics include vinyl, which is used to make records; polythene for film and containers; polyfluoroethylene used for nonstick pans, and nylon in ropes.

In thermosetting plastics, the long-chain molecules link together to prevent bending, and are hard and rigid. They include melamine, used for tableware; liquid plastics that set to hard coatings, such as polyurethane paints; and epoxy resins, which set to glue things together. Synthetic rubber is a rubber-like plastic.

MAKING LIQUID OXYGEN

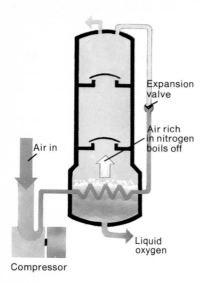

Expansion valve

Air rich in nitrogen boils off

Air in

Liquid oxygen

Compressor

▲ HOW IS LIQUID AIR PRODUCED?

To make liquid air, air has to be cooled so much that the gases in the air turn to liquids. This happens at −312°F. Air is liquefied in machines that work like refrigerators. Liquid air is kept cold in vacuum flasks.

Air is liquefied by compressing it, removing the heat produced by compression, and then making it expand. The expansion causes the temperature to drop. By doing this several times, the temperature of the air falls to −312°F and the nitrogen and oxygen gases in the air become liquid. Air is liquefied to obtain nitrogen and oxygen. By allowing liquid air to boil, the gases in the air can be separated.

Engineers can excavate ground that is waterlogged by injecting liquid nitrogen to freeze the ground solid. Liquid oxygen is also used to power space rockets. Explosives can be made by mixing a material that burns, such as sawdust, with liquid oxygen.

▼ HOW IS COAL OBTAINED?

Coal is found in layers under the ground. If the coal is near the surface, it is dug out of huge pits called strip mines. If the coal is deep underground, it is mined by digging shafts and tunnels to reach the coal.

Huge excavators are used to dig strip mines to reach the layers or seams of coal. Then the coal is broken up with explosive charges and carried to preparation plants to be washed and graded into different sizes.

In a deep coal mine, shafts are sunk to reach the coal seams. Miners travel down in a cage to the coal face. There they use cutting machines to remove the coal, which is taken by conveyor belts along tunnels to an underground railroad. Trucks carry the coal to a shaft, where it is lifted to a grading and washing plant on the surface. To keep the air fresh inside the mine, giant fans draw fresh air through the tunnels and suck out stale air. The workings may stretch many miles underground.

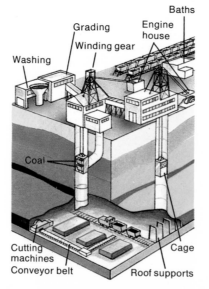

Baths

Engine house

Grading

Winding gear

Washing

Coal

Cutting machines

Conveyor belt

Cage

Roof supports

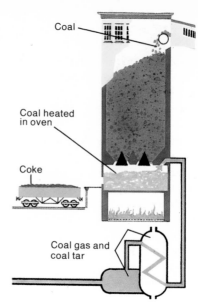

Coal

Coal heated in oven

Coke

Coal gas and coal tar

▲ HOW IS COAL USED?

People who have fire-places in their homes burn coal to heat the rooms. Coal is also used to make coal gas at gas works. This gas is piped to homes in some cities and burned in cookers and heaters. Coke and products like plastics, drugs and dyes are also made from coal.

Coke is a fuel that is made from coal by heating it in an oven so that it does not catch fire. Instead it forms coke, coal tar and coal gas. Coke is used to make iron and steel, coal tar to surface roads and coal gas to supply homes and industry.

However, coal tar and coal gas contain many useful chemicals. These are separated from the tar and gas and then used to make many kinds of products, including plastics, dyes, paints, drugs, fertilizers and insecticides.

The chemicals are also obtained by treating coal in other ways, for example, by heating it with hydrogen to give hydrocarbons, which are used as fuels and oils.

▼ HOW DOES A POWER STATION WORK?

The electricity that we use comes from a power station. It is made in the power station by a generator. Inside the generator, big magnets spin around and produce electric current in coils of wire. The generator is driven by a steam turbine (an engine). The steam is made in boilers that burn fuels such as coal or oil.

The boiler in a power station raises steam at high pressure. The boiler usually burns coal, oil or gas that is transported or piped to the power station. In nuclear power stations, the boiler is heated by a nuclear reactor instead. The steam goes to the turbine, where it spins the blades of the turbine. The steam is then piped to cooling towers, in which it condenses to water. The warm water flows from the cooling tower and returns to the boiler, so saving both water and fuel.

Inside the generator, a shaft driven by the turbine rotates an electromagnet. This electromagnet is powered by a small generator and produces a powerful magnetic field. As it spins, the magnetic field cuts across coils of wire placed around the electromagnet and produces a powerful electric current in the coils. This current then flows to a transformer, where it is increased to a high voltage and fed into the power lines.

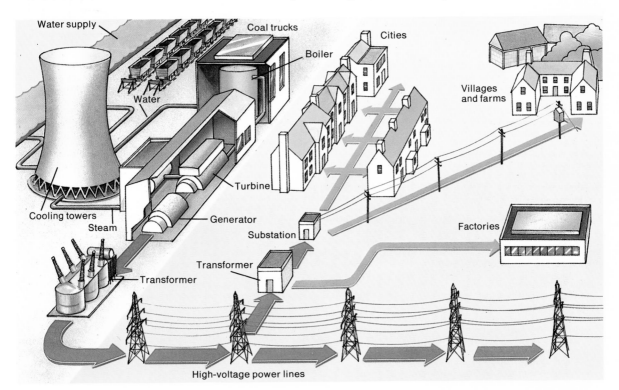

Water supply · Coal trucks · Cities · Boiler · Water · Cooling towers · Steam · Turbine · Generator · Substation · Transformer · Transformer · Villages and farms · Factories · High-voltage power lines

▲ HOW DOES ELECTRICITY REACH THE HOME?

The electric current flows out to power lines. The power lines bring the electricity to homes and factories. The current travels along overhead or underground wires. It has to go through transformers and substations, where the current is changed to the lower voltage used in homes.

As the current leaves the power station, its voltage is increased to as much as 400,000 volts or possibly more. The reason for this is that the power lines which carry the electricity lose power if it travels at low voltage, so the voltage is increased in a transformer. The current is then fed into a network of high-voltage power lines which distribute electricity throughout the surrounding region.

Before it can be used, the voltage is lowered in another transformer. Factories may take current at several thousand volts, but homes receive electric power of between 100 and 250 volts. Substations in cities and towns contain transformers to reduce the voltage. From the substations, the current travels through cables beneath the streets. In country areas overhead wires may be used.

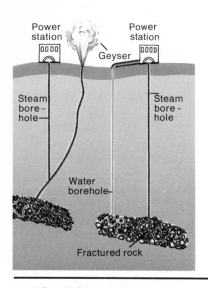

Power station   Power station

Geyser

Steam bore-hole

Steam bore-hole

Water borehole

Fractured rock

◀ HOW DO WE GET POWER FROM THE GROUND?

It is very hot inside the Earth, and in some parts of the world it is very hot near the surface. Hot water or steam may come up through vents in the rock, or through holes drilled down to the hot region. This hot water is used to warm homes, and the steam goes to power stations to make electricity.

Heat that is tapped from below ground is called geothermal power. It is used mostly in Iceland, Italy, New Zealand, Japan and the United States. These are volcanic regions where hot water and steam rise to the surface at hot springs and geysers. Other countries are looking for geothermal power.

As well as drilling down to them, it is also possible to tap the heat of hot dry rocks. Pumping water down a bore-hole to the rock fractures it and turns the water to steam. The steam then rises up a second borehole.

▶ HOW DOES A WINDMILL WORK?

Big windmills with blades like huge aircraft pro-pellors are being built to produce electricity to supply cities and towns. The blades turn a shaft that is connected to an electric generator on top of the windmill. Small windmills are used to pump water or to generate electricity for farms.

Small windmills have a vane behind the sails to catch the wind if it changes direction and turn the sails into the wind. Large windmills have an automatic control system that turns the head of the windmill into the wind.

The largest windmills have blades that are 200 feet long, and are mounted on towers about 330 feet high. The blades need to be very large and high to catch as much wind as possible. In this way, more of the energy that is in the wind is turned into elec-tricity. In the future, rows of huge windmills may line the coast in windy regions.

Wind-power generator at Gedser, Denmark

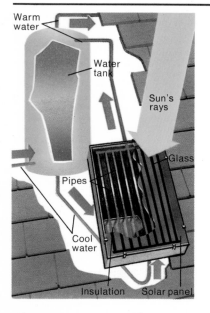

Warm water

Water tank

Sun's rays

Glass

Pipes

Cool water

Insulation   Solar panel

◀ HOW DO WE USE SOLAR POWER?

We can use the Sun's warmth to provide free heat. Solar panels on the roofs of houses trap the Sun's rays. They warm water flowing through the panels. In this way solar power helps to produce hot water for washing and heating.

Solar panels are covered with glass to trap the Sun's rays. Inside they are painted black to absorb as much heat as possible. Water runs through pipes in the panels and is warmed by the Sun's heat. The warm water goes to a tank, and it may return to the solar panels to be heated some more. In this way, the Sun's heat is used to warm the hot water supply of a house. Solar power may not be enough to heat the water fully, but it is a free source of energy and therefore reduces heating costs.

Houses may have heat exchangers and heat storage tanks so that the heat can be stored.

▼ HOW IS HYDROELECTRIC POWER MADE?

Hydroelectric power is a kind of electricity. It is made in power stations at waterfalls or high dams. Water falling down pipes to the power station drives generators. The electricity they produce goes to homes and factories. It is no different from the electricity produced by other kinds of power stations.

Hydroelectric power stations can only work where water falls a long way. This is so that the water gains enough power to drive the electricity generators in the power station. A high dam may therefore be built to store up the water in a large reservoir above the power station. The station contains turbines in which the stream of falling water drives paddle-shaped blades round. A shaft connected to the blades then powers the generators as in ordinary power stations.

Hydroelectric stations continue to work at night, when little electricity is needed. To prevent this waste of power, the turbines in some hydroelectric power stations are fed with power at night to act as pumps. They pump water up to the reservoir above the station. The station then uses this water to generate power during the day.

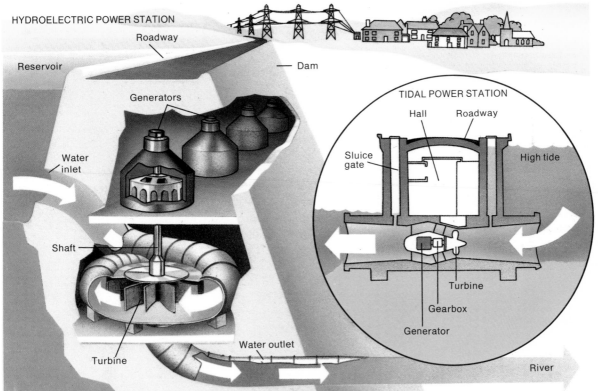

HYDROELECTRIC POWER STATION
Roadway
Reservoir
Dam
Generators
Water inlet
Shaft
Turbine
Water outlet
River

TIDAL POWER STATION
Hall
Roadway
Sluice gate
High tide
Turbine
Gearbox
Generator

▲ HOW DO WE GET POWER FROM THE SEA?

We can get power from the sea by using the tides. As the tides rise and fall, water flows in and out of river mouths. The water can be used to drive electricity generators in a barrage (a kind of dam) built across the river. There is a tidal power station at the mouth of the River Rance in France.

Like hydroelectric power stations, tidal power stations do not use any fuel. They are therefore very cheap to run, but they cost a lot to build. Tidal power stations do not produce much power when the tide is changing. So, at times of low power demand, a tidal power station may use power to pump water into the river mouth from the sea so that it can be used later when power is required.

Tidal power stations can only be built where there is a large rise and fall in water level caused by the tides. This occurs in narrow river estuaries, straits and bays. Not many sites are suitable for tidal power stations, so it is unlikely that many will be built to follow the Rance tidal station in France, the world's first. Possible sites include the Severn estuary in England and the Bay of Fundy in Canada, where the tides can rise and fall by 50 feet.

▼ WHAT IS CEMENT MADE OF?

Cement is usually made from limestone and clay, but chalk and sand may also be used. These materials are fed into a big machine that crushes them into small pieces and mixes them. Then the mixture is heated in a kiln. When it cools, it is ground into cement powder.

The principal minerals in cement are lime, which comes mainly from limestone, and silica and alumina, which are provided by clay. Some iron ore is also used. After crushing and blending, the various ingredients are fed into a rotating kiln and heated to about 2730°C for several hours. This heating produces a clinker that is then ground to a powder with a mineral called gypsum. This is added to regulate the time that the cement takes to harden. Adding water to the cement powder makes the minerals combine together, producing a firm bond as the cement hardens.

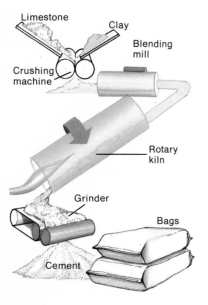

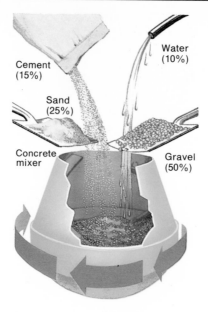

▲ HOW IS CONCRETE MADE?

Concrete is made by mixing gravel or small stones, sand and cement together with water. These materials are placed in a revolving concrete mixer, or they can be mixed together with a spade. The concrete is a paste that sets to form a hard material. It is used in building to make floors and walls, as well as roads, bridges and dams.

Most concrete is made in a concrete mixer, which revolves to turn the ingredients over and over so that they mix thoroughly. The mixer is up-ended and the concrete poured out. It is then carried or piped into a mold, where the concrete sets hard in the shape of the mold. Slabs, blocks and pipes are made in this way, and constructions can be built in any shape required by using concrete. However, concrete is not very strong and has to be strengthened, often by placing steel bars in the concrete to reinforce it.

▼ HOW ARE SKYSCRAPERS BUILT?

Skyscrapers are tall buildings that tower in the air. First, holes are dug in the ground so that the skyscraper is firmly fixed in place by its underground foundations. Then a high frame is built up from the foundations. Finally, walls and floors are fixed to the frame.

The foundations of a skyscraper are laid by drilling holes in the ground and filling them with concrete. If the ground is firm, the foundations are wide so that they will spread the weight of the building and they do not go very deep. If the ground is not very firm, deep shafts of concrete are driven into the ground to anchor the skyscraper firmly.

Then a frame of steel girders or concrete beams is erected, often with a pillar-like concrete core containing elevator shafts and stairs. The frame and core take all the weight of the building so that the walls do not have to support the floors above.

▶ HOW ARE TALL BUILDINGS AND SMOKE-STACKS DEMOLISHED?

Demolition experts who knock down high buildings and smokestacks must make sure that they will not fall on other buildings nearby. Sometimes, they have to take the building or smokestack apart piece by piece. But to save time, they may be able to blow it up instead.

To make a building collapse so that it falls straight down without tipping over, experts place explosives throughout the building. When the charges are fired, all the walls collapse at the same time. Before demolishing the building, the beams supporting it are weakened so that none of the walls fall outward. A smokestock can be made to fall in a particular direction by first making a hole in one side of the base while supporting the stack with posts. By setting fire to the posts or knocking them away, the stack will topple over in this direction.

▼ HOW ARE TUNNELS BUILT?

Many tunnels are dug with tunneling machines called moles. These are like huge drills that cut a shaft through the ground. At the head of the mole, rotating cutters dig out the rock or soil, which is carried away along a conveyor belt. Powerful jacks act like springs to force the mole forward as it removes the rock and soil ahead.

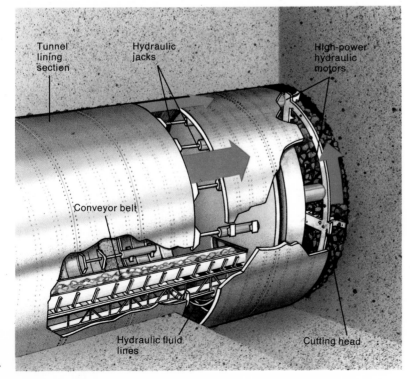

Tunnel lining section

Hydraulic jacks

High-power hydraulic motors

Conveyor belt

Hydraulic fluid lines

Cutting head

As the mole edges forward through the ground, engineers fix lining panels into place to form the walls of the tunnel. For power and safety, the mole is driven by electric motors and hydraulic jacks, which are fed with high-pressure fluid along lines from the surface.

In good conditions, a mole can burrow through the ground at 16 feet an hour for a train-sized tunnel. Progress may be slow when the soil is waterlogged, as the water or soft soil tends to flow into the tunnel. To prevent this happening, the head of the mole is contained in a sealed compartment.

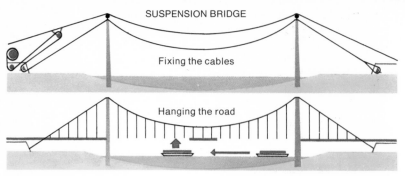

SUSPENSION BRIDGE

Fixing the cables

Hanging the road

▲ HOW ARE BRIDGES BUILT?

Most bridges rest on supports called piers. A wall is built in the river to keep out the water, and the piers are fixed in the bed of the river. Then the bridge is built on the piers. When it is finished, some of the piers may be taken away. Suspension bridges are built by fixing cables across a river from high towers on each side. The road is then hung from the main cables.

Long bridges need to be supported between the piers that hold them up. Arches carry a bridge by transferring its weight to the supports at each end of the arches. Frames of girders may be built above or below the road or railroad to strengthen the bridge.

Cantilever bridges are made in two sections, each supported on a pier near each end of the bridge. The sections meet in the middle of the bridge, giving a long span.

▶ HOW DOES A JACK-HAMMER WORK?

Jackhammers are used to break through the road surface and dig up the road. The jackhammer has a strong blade like a chisel that strikes the road many times a second. It is driven by compressed air piped to the jackhammer from a compressor.

Jackhammers are also called pneumatic drills because they work on compressed air. As the air enters the drill, the diaphragm valve first lets the air into the base of the piston, forcing it upwards. This action causes the valve to rock and send air to the top of the piston, which moves down and strikes the blade of the drill.

The air then leaves through the exhaust, and the valve rocks back to admit more air to the base of the piston again. The whole action is then repeated.

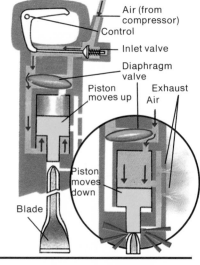

Air (from compressor)
Control
Inlet valve
Diaphragm valve
Piston moves up
Exhaust Air
Piston moves down
Blade

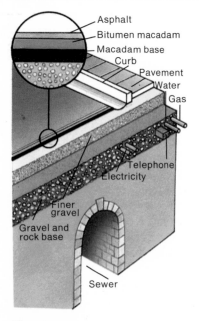

Asphalt
Bitumen macadam
Macadam base
Curb
Pavement
Water
Gas
Telephone
Electricity
Finer gravel
Gravel and rock base
Sewer

◀ HOW ARE ROADS BUILT?

To build a road, engineers first make the ground level. Then they construct a base of stones or gravel, on which they put a layer of concrete or macadam (crushed rock mixed with clay or tar). Finally a layer of tar called bitumen or asphalt is usually spread on top. The road builders also make drains at the side of the road to carry away rainwater.

Highways have to be hard-wearing to carry heavy traffic. They are often made of concrete, usually with a surface of tough bitumen. Roads in towns do not carry such heavy traffic, and are generally made of gravel and macadam and surfaced with asphalt and chippings. These roads can be easily dug up to get to the service pipes beneath. These include drains to carry off rainwater, electricity and telephone cables, and pipes containing water and gas. Beneath these pipes are sewers which carry wastes from buildings to sewage disposal plants or to a river or the sea.

▶ HOW DO ROBOTS WORK?

Most robots consist of a mechanical arm with a gripper like a pair of tongs at one end. Inside the arm are hydraulic motors that can move the arm and gripper in any direction. The arm is connected to a box of controls that operate the motors to make the robot perform a particular action.

The controls of the robot are able to move its arm and gripper to exactly the same positions every time the robot performs a certain task.

The robot is first taught the various movements that it must make. A human operator uses the controls to make the robot perform the action. The controls contain a memory like a computer memory that remembers all the arm and gripper positions. They can then direct the robot to carry out this action over and over again with perfect precision. A new action can be fed into the memory to make the robot carry out a different task.

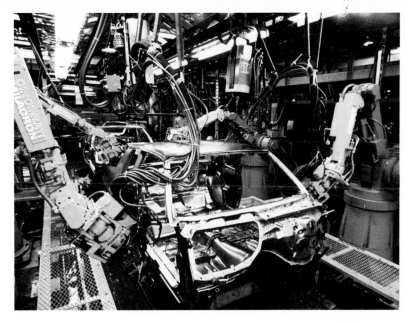

▲ WHAT ARE ROBOTS USED FOR?

Robots are mainly used to do jobs that involve carrying out the same action over and over again. These are jobs like painting and welding, and loading and unloading parts in factories and taking them from one place to another.

Robots are used in industries such as car manufacturing because they can repeat the same task as many times as required without making a mistake. The jobs they do are fairly simple, like spraying paint in the same pattern over each car body that comes to them, or welding the same parts of the body together.

As robots improve, they will even be able to check the jobs that they are doing. Some robots already have vision and touch sensors. They make parts for products and assemble them.

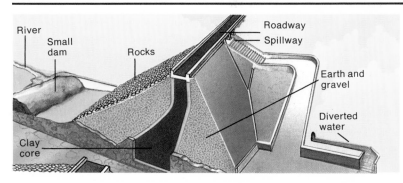

River
Small dam
Rocks
Roadway
Spillway
Earth and gravel
Diverted water
Clay core

▲ HOW ARE DAMS BUILT?

A dam is a huge barrier built across a valley so that river water piles up behind it to form a lake. Many dams are constructed by heaping up earth and rock, while others are made of concrete or stone blocks. While the dam is being built, the river is diverted around the site. A small dam or wall is built to send the water to one side.

An earth-fill dam is made with a solid core of clay surrounded by earth and gravel and covered with rocks. A central wall may be needed to stop water seeping through the dam. Like some dams made of concrete or stone, they are so big that their weight keeps them in place.

Buttress dams are thin dams built with supports called buttresses to hold them up. Arch dams have high narrow walls that are curved. The water presses the dam into the sides of the valley, and this stops it from giving way.

▶ HOW IS LEATHER MADE?

Real leather is made from the hides or skins of animals. Cattle hides are used to make most leather. Other animals that provide leather include pigs, sheep, goats and also sharks and snakes. To make leather, the hair or fur is removed and then the hides or skins are tanned to stop them from rotting.

Hair or fur is removed from the hides or skins by soaking them in lime solution and scraping them. Most leather is then tanned in solutions containing tannin, which is obtained from plants. The tannin combines with the protein in the hide or skin.

Some leather is tanned with chemicals instead. After dyeing, the leather is treated with oil or grease to make it flexible.

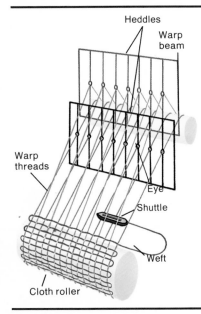

◀ HOW IS CLOTH WOVEN?

Much cloth is made by weaving threads together. A loom is used for weaving. Lines of threads called warp threads move up and down in the loom. In between each movement, a shuttle pulls another thread called the weft between the warp threads. This action weaves the warp and weft threads together.

The warp threads are wound on a roller called the warp beam. They then pass through holes called eyes in frames of wires called heddles. The frames move up and down as the shuttle passes to and fro. In this way, the weft thread passes alternately above and below the warp threads, weaving a pattern. To get different patterns, the warp threads move up and down in different arrangements. A roller pulls the warp threads through the loom, and the cloth winds on to the roller as it turns. Power looms and hand looms work in basically the same way.

▶ HOW DOES A ZIPPER WORK?

Metal zippers have lines of tiny teeth, while plastic zippers contain small loops on each side. When you pull the slide of the zipper up, it pushes the teeth or loops together.

Beneath each tooth in a metal zipper is a small space. The slide is narrow at the bottom so that it forces the teeth together as you pull up the zipper. The teeth on one side fit between the teeth on the other side. As they come together, each tooth slots into the space under the tooth above and the zipper stays closed. As the slide moves down, a divider at the top of the slide pulls the teeth apart.

Top pieces and a bottom piece at the ends of the fastener stop the slide coming off, though some zippers are designed to separate completely by pulling one line of teeth out of the bottom piece. Plastic zippers have two spiral coils instead of lines of teeth, but they work in the same way.

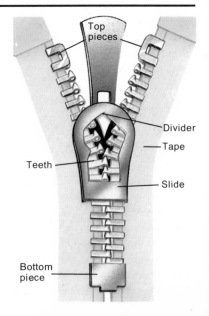

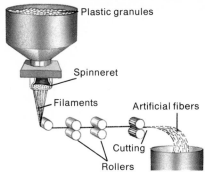

Plastic granules

Spinneret

Filaments

Artificial fibers

Cutting

Rollers

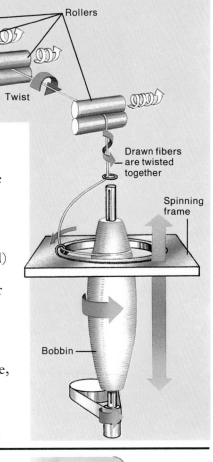

Sliver of natural or artificial fibers

Rollers

Twist

Drawn fibers are twisted together

Spinning frame

Bobbin

▲ HOW ARE TEXTILE FIBERS SPUN?

Textiles like cloth are made with thread or yarn, which come from fibers. Natural fibers are plant or animal hairs, while artificial fibers are made of plastic. The fibers are combed loosely together to form a strip of fibers called a sliver. Then the sliver is rolled and twisted to make the thread or yarn.

Artificial fibers are made from plastic granules, which are melted and forced through holes in a spinneret to produce filaments. These are drawn through rollers and then cut to make fibers.

To spin thread, a sliver of either artificial or natural fibers (such as cotton or wool) is drawn through rollers. These rotate faster and faster to pull out the fibers in the sliver. The fibers are also twisted and link together to produce the thread or yarn. This goes to a spinning frame, where the thread is twisted again as it is wound on to a bobbin. The thread is then ready to be woven into cloth.

▶ HOW IS POTTERY MADE?

Pottery includes containers like bowls and mugs and objects like tiles that are all made of clay. The pots and other articles are first formed in soft wet clay. Then the pottery is heated in a kiln.

Many potters use a wheel that is powered by a foot treadle to shape clay. They control the wheel with one foot as they shape the pot between their thumbs and fingers. Handles and spouts are made separately and stuck to the pot using very soft clay. Other kinds of pottery are made by cutting or molding the clay into shape.

Before the pottery is fired in the kiln, it is dried. Then a glaze may be added. When the glaze is fired, it produces a shiny coating on the pottery. Often, the glaze is added after the pot is fired, so that a second firing is required to glaze the pottery. The glaze may also give the pottery a certain color, or the pottery may be painted before or after glazing.

The finest pottery is called porcelain or china. It is white, but some light shines through the porcelain. One of the main ingredients of porcelain is kaolin, or China clay.

Pottery is also made in great quantities in factories. Machines press and mold the clay into shape. Glazing and decorating may also be done automatically.

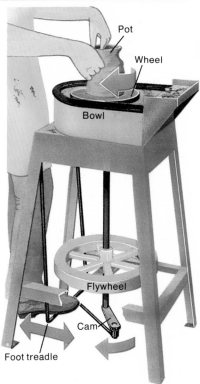

Pot

Wheel

Bowl

Flywheel

Cam

Foot treadle

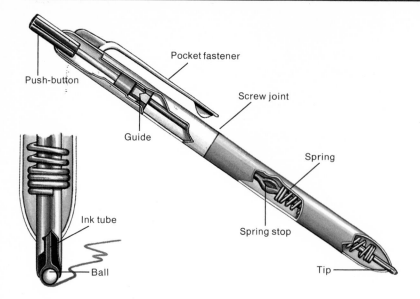

Push-button
Pocket fastener
Screw joint
Guide
Spring
Ink tube
Spring stop
Ball
Tip

▲ HOW DOES A BALLPOINT PEN WORK?

Inside a ballpoint pen is a thin tube of ink. At the tip of the tube is an opening with a tiny ball in it. When you write, the ball spins as the tip moves over the paper. The ink sticks to the ball and then flows onto the paper.

The ink that is used in a ballpoint pen is special ink that dries as soon as it meets the air. This means that the writing will not smudge. In addition, the ink dries on the ball at the tip of the pen as soon as it is lifted from the paper. The dry ink seals the opening at the tip of the pen, and the ink inside cannot flow out or dry up inside.

Many ballpoint pens have push-button actions that push the ink tube forward for writing and retract it when the pen is not in use. The push-button operates a guide that rotates to force the tube up or down, and a spring holds it in position.

◄ HOW IS INK MADE?

The kind of ink used with fountain pens is often made by mixing water with colored pigments or dyes. It takes some time to dry because the water has to evaporate and leave the pigment or dye on the paper. The kind of ink in coloring pens and ballpoint pens contains dyes or pigments mixed with liquids that dry very quickly.

Pigments are colored powders that lie on the surface of the paper. Dyes are colored materials that penetrate the surface and color the paper itself.

Inks used for printing are made by mixing pigments with special oils or varnishes that help to bind the pigment to the paper. Carbon black is a black pigment that is often used to make black printing ink. It is a fine black powder similar to soot. Colored pigments used in printing inks and the dyes in other kinds of inks are made from chemicals.

▶ HOW DOES AN ERASER WORK?

You can remove pencil marks from paper with an eraser or rubber. The pencil puts a layer of graphite particles on the surface of the paper. The particles are sticky, and attach themselves to the eraser as it moves over the paper.

A soft eraser stays clean because its surface rubs away as it is used. To remove deep pencil marks and also ink marks, a hard eraser can be

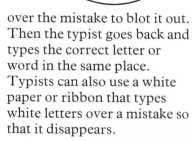

Eraser
Graphite particles
Paper

used. This does not pick up the pencil or ink markings. Instead, it rubs away the top surface of the paper.

Typists can correct mistakes in typing in other ways. A special white paint that dries quickly can be spread over the mistake to blot it out. Then the typist goes back and types the correct letter or word in the same place. Typists can also use a white paper or ribbon that types white letters over a mistake so that it disappears.

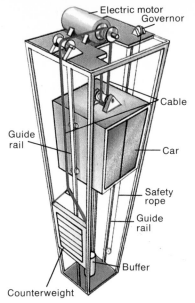

▲ HOW DOES AN ELEVATOR WORK?

The car of the elevator that carries people up and down hangs from one end of a cable. An electric motor turns a drive pulley that winds the cable up and down. At the other end of the cable is a big weight called a counterweight. This is as heavy as the car and balances it.

The counterweight balances the weight of the car so that the motor has to raise and lower only the weight of the people inside the elevator. The car runs between guide rails up and down the shaft. Controls inside the car operate the motor to take the car to any floor.

A safety device called a governor stops a car from falling if the cable breaks. A safety rope connected to the car turns the governor, and if it moves too quickly the governor operates a switch that makes the car grip the guide rails and stop. Even if this does not work, a buffer at the bottom of the elevator shaft will break the car's fall.

▼ HOW DOES AN ESCALATOR WORK?

Escalators are the moving stairs that carry people up and down in places like big shops. They move as fast as 13 feet a second. The steps of the escalator are connected by an endless chain that goes around and around without stopping. At the end, the steps go underneath the escalator and back to the beginning.

The steps of the escalator have wheels which run on rails under the steps. In the sloping part of the escalator, the rails are situated beside each other so that the steps are raised one above or below the other like a staircase.

Near the top and bottom, the steps level out so that people can walk on or off the escalator. Here, the rails move apart so that the tops of the steps line up with each other. The motor that drives the chain connecting the steps together also drives the handrail through a set of gears.

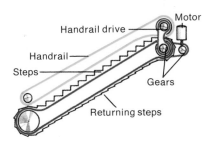

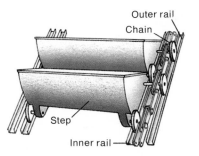

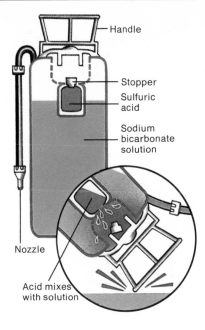

▲ HOW DOES A FIRE EXTINGUISHER WORK?

To put out a fire, the extinguisher sprays out liquid or a vapor or foam. This cools the fire and also covers it to stop air from getting to the fire. One common type of fire extinguisher sprays water. Gas produced inside the extinguisher forces the water out.

Inside a water-filled extinguisher is a bottle of sulfuric acid and a solution of sodium bicarbonate. To use this extinguisher, you turn it upside down or strike a knob. This action either opens or breaks the bottle of acid, and it mixes with the bicarbonate solution. Immediately, a large amount of carbon dioxide gas is released inside the extinguisher, forcing the solution out of the nozzle in a powerful jet.

To fight fires caused by electrical faults or burning chemicals, water is not used. Instead, firemen have extinguishers that spray a heavy vapor or a smothering foam.

▲ HOW ARE NEWSPAPERS PRINTED?

Newspapers are printed on huge presses that can print millions of papers. Giant rolls of paper are fed into the presses. The complete paper is then printed on one length of paper, and the machine then cuts this up into sections and folds them together.

In many newspapers, the printers use machines to set the articles in whole lines of type. The lines are then fitted in frames, together with printing blocks containing the pictures, to make the pages.

Molds are then made of the pages, and several curved printing plates are made from each mold. In many papers, the printing plates are made by electronic and photographic methods. The plates are then fitted on to the printing cylinders so that each press can print a complete paper.

▶ WHAT IS PAPER MADE FROM?

Most paper is made from wood. It consists of fibers (tiny pieces) of wood tangled together. Some paper comes from rags. Wood and rags are treated with water to make a paste called pulp. The pulp is then spread to form a layer, which is dried to make paper.

Paper is made in huge factories called paper mills. Inside the mill, logs are ground up with huge wheels and mixed with water to make pulp. Pulp is also made by chopping up rags or wood and heating them with chemicals. The pulp is then bleached white and additives are mixed in. For example, glue is added to make the fibers stick together in the paper. Then the pulp is spread out on a belt of wire mesh. The water is sucked away through the holes in the mesh and the pulp

forms a sheet of paper. Then the paper goes through rollers to dry it and smooth its surface.

Different kinds of paper, like tissue paper and writing paper, are made with different kinds of pulp.

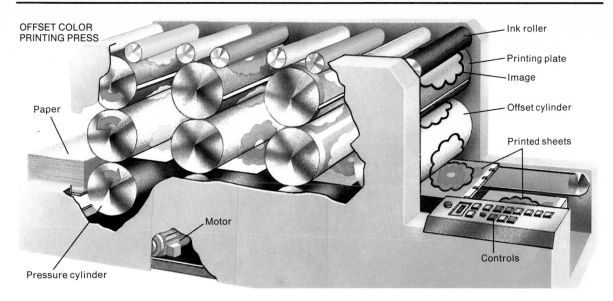

OFFSET COLOR PRINTING PRESS

Ink roller

Printing plate

Image

Offset cylinder

Printed sheets

Paper

Motor

Controls

Pressure cylinder

▲ HOW DOES A COLOR PRINTING PRESS WORK?

Even though they look multicolored, the color pictures in books and magazines are printed in only four colors. The press prints the picture separately in red, yellow, blue and black. These four colored pictures overlap and we see the picture in full color.

The printing press has four printing plates that are fixed to cylinders. Each plate has an image of the picture on it. The plates are made from red, yellow, blue and black-and-white photographs of the picture that is being printed.

As each cylinder rotates, ink is fed to the plate and taken up by the image on the plate. This cylinder then turns to print the image on the paper. The paper passes through four sets of cylinders, and the four images build up to give a full-color picture. In offset printing, the image is transferred to an offset cylinder, which then prints it on the paper.

▶ HOW ARE BOOKS BOUND?

Binding a book means putting the pages together and fitting its cover. The pages come in sections like thin books. The sections are placed in order and sewn together with strong thread. The cover is then glued on to the back and sides of the book.

Separate endpapers are often attached to the book when the page sections are sewn together. The back is then glued to keep the pages in place, and the pages are trimmed with knives to make them even. Then the book is placed in a frame and the back hammered to round it, and a lining is glued to the back to

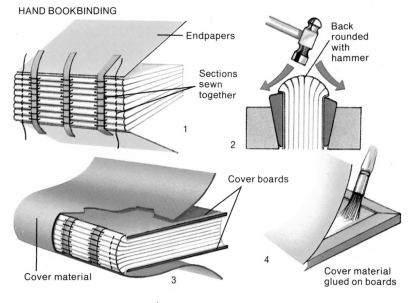

HAND BOOKBINDING

Endpapers

Sections sewn together

1

Back rounded with hammer

2

Cover boards

Cover material

3

4

Cover material glued on boards

reinforce it.

The case or cover is then attached to the book. This may involve glueing boards to the endpapers and then covering the boards and back with cloth or leather. The title and author's name is then stamped on the cover.

Alternatively, the whole cover is made separately and then fixed to the endpapers.

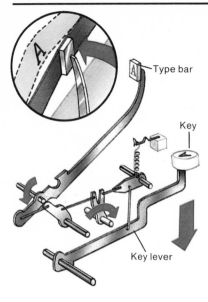

Type bar

Key

Key lever

▲ HOW DOES A TYPE-WRITER WORK?

A typewriter has a set of keys marked with letters, numbers and signs. When you press a key, it marks the paper held against the cylinder. A type bar connected to the key strikes an inked ribbon, and the ribbon marks the paper. A spring then pulls the cylinder, moving the paper along to the next position.

A system of levers and springs connects each key to its type bar. Each type bar has two letters (one capital letter and one small letter) or a number and a sign or two signs. The typist selects one of these by pressing a shift key that raises or lowers the type bars. In electric typewriters, an electric motor moves the type bars and cylinder.

A golf-ball typewriter does not have type bars. Instead, all the letters, numbers and signs are mounted on a round typing head shaped like a golf ball. Pressing a key rotates the head to the correct position and the head strikes the ribbon.

▼ HOW DOES A TELEPRINTER WORK?

A teleprinter is a kind of typewriter that is used to send written messages by telephone. Instead of speaking on the telephone, a message is typed out on the teleprinter. The letters are changed into electric signals, which go along the telephone wires to a teleprinter at the other end. This types out the message.

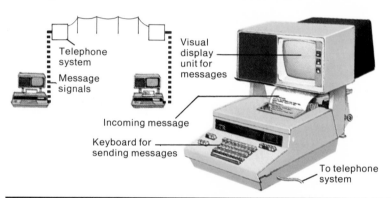

Telephone system

Message signals

Visual display unit for messages

Incoming message

Keyboard for sending messages

To telephone system

▼ HOW DOES A CALCULATOR DISPLAY NUMBERS?

The numbers on a calculator's display are all made of straight lines in different patterns. All of them seen together give 8.

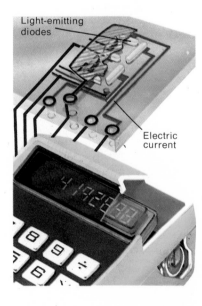

Light-emitting diodes

Electric current

The telephone system used for connecting teleprinters is known as *Telex*. Any teleprinter in the Telex network can be reached simply by dialling its number. Telex is useful when a written record of a message is needed.

However, the system is likely to use computers more and more. Computers can be connected together by telephone, and messages can be sent between computers far more quickly than between teleprinters.

Wires connect each of these lines to the calculator's electronic brain. Electric signals go to the display, and light up some of the lines to produce numbers.

Calculators have two different kinds of displays. LED displays have numbers that glow brightly, usually in red. The displays which do not glow but show up rather like numbers on paper are called LCD displays. LED stands for *light-emitting diodes*. These glow when an electric current is fed to them.

LCD stands for *liquid crystal displays*. These displays use up very little electric power. The lines in each number contain liquid crystals, which pass or block light depending on an electric signal fed to them.

▶ HOW DOES A PHOTOCOPIER WORK?

A photocopier makes instant copies of pages of books and other documents. You place the page on a glass plate and press a button. The page is lit up from inside the machine. An image of the page is then produced, made of particles of dark powder.

There are two main kinds of photocopiers. Xerographic copiers use ordinary paper while electrostatic copiers require special coated paper.

Inside a xerographic copier, an image of the page is projected onto a revolving drum with a light-sensitive surface. The image charges the surface of the drum to give a pattern of electric charge. The drum is then dusted with a powder called a toner and the powder clings to the charged parts of the surface, producing a dark image of the original page on the drum. A sheet of paper is then rolled against the drum, and the powder image transfers to the paper. Finally, the paper is heated to bake the powder.

In electrostatic copiers, the image of the page is projected directly on to the paper, which charges its surface. The paper then passes through a bath of toner, and the particles cling to the charged parts of the paper to produce the copy.

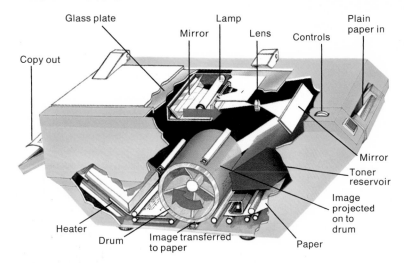

XEROGRAPHIC COPIER

Glass plate · Lamp · Plain paper in · Mirror · Lens · Controls · Copy out · Mirror · Toner reservoir · Image projected on to drum · Heater · Drum · Image transferred to paper · Paper

▼ WHAT DOES A WORD PROCESSOR DO?

A word processor is a kind of electronic typewriter. You type in words and they appear on a screen.

Then the processor types all the words onto paper automatically. It types as many copies as required, and you can make changes without having to type everything out again.

The word processor is in fact a kind of computer. It has a memory which stores all the words that you type into it at the keyboard. Then, whenever required, the processor fetches the words from its memory and sends them to its typing unit to be typed onto paper. This has many advantages. You see the words you have typed on the screen first, so you can check that there are no mistakes. The processor can then type a perfect letter or whatever document you require, and produce copies.

It can also make changes automatically. This is useful for typing the same letter to many people, but with a different name and address on each letter. In future, the word processor's memory may also be able to check spelling.

▼ HOW DO YOU GET SOUND FROM A BRASS INSTRUMENT?

To play a brass instrument such as a trumpet, you put your lips onto the mouthpiece. Then you close your lips tightly and blow air through the middle of them. Your lips vibrate, and this vibration sets the air in the trumpet vibrating and gives a sound. Other brass instruments include the trombone, horn, tuba, bugle and euphonium.

To get different notes on most brass instruments, you press keys or valves. This opens or closes sections of tubing in the instrument, making the length of the column of air inside the instrument get longer or shorter. This makes the note get lower or higher in pitch. However, there are usually only three keys or valves, and pressing all combinations of these gives only seven notes. A trombone has a slide that the player moves in and out to get notes, but it too cannot produce more than seven notes.

To get more notes, the brass player tightens his or her lips. Without using the valves or slide, a brass player can get a set of notes called harmonics. These are the notes played in bugle calls, because a bugle has no valves. Good players can get very high notes in this way.

To get the notes that lie in between the harmonics, the player uses the keys, valves or slide. Hitting the right note on a brass instrument is a combination of the right lip pressure and the correct key, valve or slide position.

▲ HOW ARE WOODWIND INSTRUMENTS PLAYED?

To get a sound from a woodwind instrument like the clarinet, you put the mouthpiece into your mouth and blow. This sets the column of air inside the instrument vibrating and a note comes out. You also finger the keys on the instrument to open and close holes along the side, and get different notes.

Not all woodwind instruments are made of wood. The saxophone is made of metal, and so too are many flutes. The various instruments also have different kinds of mouthpieces. In the piccolo and flute, the player blows air across a hole in the side of the instrument. This makes the edges of the hole vibrate, which set the air column in the tube of the instrument sounding. The recorder is similar, but the player blows into a mouthpiece which sends the air across the edge of a hole in the tube.

The other woodwind instruments have mouthpieces that contain stiff reeds. Blowing into the mouthpiece sets the reed vibrating and this makes the air column in the instrument sound. The clarinet and saxophone have a single reed, whereas the oboe, English horn and bassoon contain a double reed.

To get different notes, the fingers open and close holes in the instrument or operate keys that move pads over the holes up or down. This action changes the length of the air column vibrating inside the instrument.

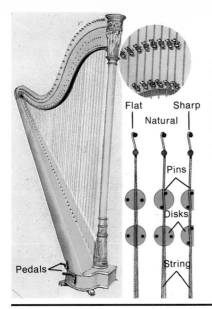

Flat | Sharp
Natural
Pins
Disks
Pedals
String

◄ WHY DOES A HARPIST USE PEDALS?

If you watch an orchestra in action, you will see the harpist pressing pedals on the harp as well as playing the strings. Moving the pedals up and down gives the harpist more notes. The pedals turn small disks with pins that grip the strings.

The kind of harp played in orchestras does not have enough strings to play all the notes that are needed. It can only play a scale of notes that is rather like the white notes on the piano.

To get the other notes (like the black notes), the harpist has to press the pedals. The disks turn so that the pins make the lengths of string vibrate shorter or longer, giving sharp or flat notes.

There are seven pedals, one for each note of the scale from A to G. Moving the D pedal to sharp, for example, changes all the D strings to D sharp. To help find the right notes, some of the strings have colors.

► HOW DO STRING INSTRUMENTS MAKE A SOUND?

String instruments have tight strings that make a sound. When you play the guitar, you pluck the strings with your fingers. The other main string instruments are the violin, viola, cello and double bass. These instruments are usually played with a bow.

All string instruments give a sound when the strings vibrate. Plucking the strings sets them vibrating for a short time. When a bow is moved across a string, the rough surface of the hairs in the bow keeps it vibrating. Plucking harder or pushing the bow down make the vibration stronger and the sound gets louder.

The sound that the strings make is not very loud. The vibration of the strings sets the hollow body of the instrument vibrating too, making the sound louder.

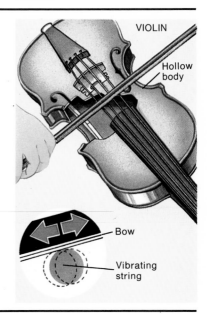

VIOLIN
Hollow body
Bow
Vibrating string

◄ HOW DOES AN ORGAN MAKE SOUNDS?

When the organist presses the keys on a pipe organ, air is blown into some of the pipes of the organ. Each pipe gives out a different note. Pipe organs are the organs seen in churches. Electric organs produce sounds from loudspeakers.

In a pipe organ, the flow of air is usually produced by an electric fan. When a key is pressed, it operates a valve to let the air into a set of pipes. The air flows over the edge of a hole cut in a pipe or over a brass reed in the pipe. These vibrate and set the column of air in the pipe vibrating so that it makes a sound.

Pipes of different sizes give different notes. The organist pushes buttons called stops to send the air to particular sets of pipes to get different sounds. In electric organs, the keys are like switches that turn on electronic sound generators. These generate electric signals that go to a loudspeaker.

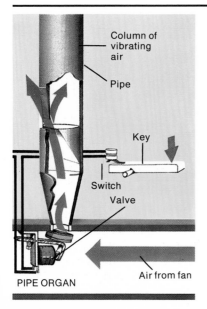

Column of vibrating air
Pipe
Key
Switch
Valve
Air from fan
PIPE ORGAN

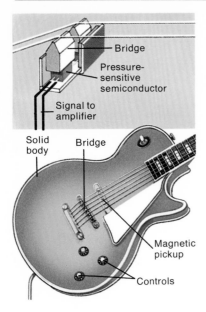

▲ HOW DOES AN ELECTRIC GUITAR WORK?

An electric guitar has strings like an ordinary guitar. However, the strings do not produce the sound. When a string is played, it makes a pickup under the strings give an electric signal. The signal goes to an amplifier and a loudspeaker, which produces the sound.

Because the strings do not produce the sound, an electric guitar can be solid. The strings are made of metal.

In guitars with magnetic pickups, the metal strings vibrate above magnets in the pickup. This causes the magnetic fields of the magnets to vary, producing an electric signal in coils surrounding the magnets.

A pressure-sensitive pickup is fixed to the strings at the bridge of some guitars. It vibrates as the strings vibrate and produces an electric signal. The strength of the signal depends on how hard the strings are played, so that the guitarist can make the music louder or softer.

▶ HOW IS AN ACOUSTIC GUITAR MADE?

An acoustic guitar is made of wood, and the best guitars are made by hand. The body of the guitar is hollow. Supports send the vibration of the strings throughout the body and make it sound too. This sound comes from the body through the sound hole under the strings.

Six strings made of metal or nylon are fixed to the bridge of the guitar. These are threaded through pegs in the machine head, and the nuts tighten up the strings until they are in tune.

The neck of the guitar is made of solid wood across which metal strips called frets are fixed. The frets form the fingerboard, which the guitarist uses to press the strings against the frets and get the notes required. An acoustic guitar can be turned into an electric guitar by attaching a pickup to it.

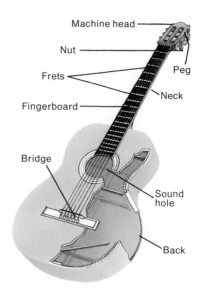

▶ HOW DOES A SYNTHESIZER WORK?

A synthesizer produces electronic music. You can use the controls to make many different sounds. This is because the synthesizer can create electric signals that make these sounds come from a loudspeaker connected to the synthesizer.

The synthesizer can imitate other instruments or make a wide range of sounds of its own. Most synthesizers are played with keyboards, but you first have to set the controls to get the particular sound you want.

The controls operate the electronic circuits inside the synthesizer. The circuits produce electric signals that vary in strength in the same way that sound waves vary in strength. The signals go to an

amplifier, and then to a loudspeaker. The signals make the loudspeaker cone vibrate, and it produces sound waves with the right kind of sound.

Instead of a keyboard, a computer can be used to operate a synthesizer. The computer is first programmed with the music.

▶ HOW DOES A PIANO WORK?

When you press piano keys, hammers move forward and strike the strings. The hammers have heads of felt, and the strings are made of taut wire. The hammers make the strings vibrate to produce sound. Dampers move against the strings when you take your fingers off the keys, and the strings stop sounding.

Connected to each key of the piano is a mechanism called the action. It consists of a set of wooden levers. When the key is pressed down, it raises a jack that moves the hammer to strike the string.

At the same time, the damper moves away from the string so that it is free to vibrate the sound. A check keeps the hammer near the string so that it is ready to strike the string again quickly if the key is pressed again without being released first. When the key is released, the jack moves down and the hammer falls away from the string sounding.

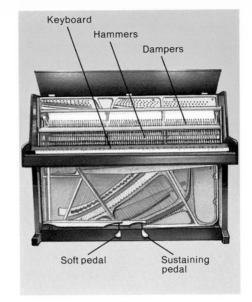

Keyboard
Hammers
Dampers
Soft pedal
Sustaining pedal

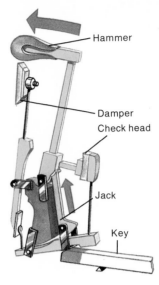

Hammer
Damper
Check head
Jack
Key

▲ WHAT DO THE PEDALS ON A PIANO DO?

Most pianos have two pedals. The left pedal makes the music softer. The right pedal makes the sounds of the notes carry on when you take your fingers off the keys. It is called the sustaining pedal.

The soft pedal works in various ways. It often moves the hammers for the middle and lower notes slightly to one side. These notes each have two or three strings. Pressing the soft pedal makes the hammers strike only one string, making the sound softer.

On other pianos, all the hammers are moved nearer the strings. When the keys are pressed, the hammers do not have to move so far to strike them. They therefore hit the strings with less force and give less sound. When the sustaining pedal is pressed, all the dampers move away from the strings. The strings continue to sound until the notes die away.

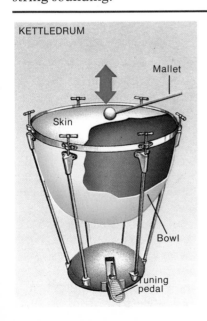

KETTLEDRUM

Mallet
Skin
Bowl
Tuning pedal

◀ HOW DO DRUMS MAKE A SOUND?

A skin is stretched over the frame of the drum. When you hit the drum, the skin vibrates and gives a sound. It also sets the frame and the air inside the frame vibrating too, and their sounds mix with the sound of the skin.

The kind of sound a drum makes depends on how you hit it. Using a drumstick gives a harsh crack, while using your hands or a soft mallet gives more of a thump. The sound also depends on the size of the drum. A bigger skin gives a deeper or more booming sound and a smaller skin a higher tone.

A snare drum has two skins with a set of wires that can be fixed against the lower skin. The wires rattle against the lower skin when the upper skin is struck, giving a bright edge to the sound.

Timpani or kettledrums are played in orchestras. These drums can produce different notes by tightening or loosening the skin.

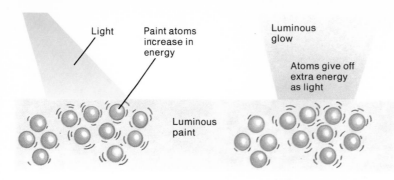

Light — Paint atoms increase in energy — Luminous paint

Luminous glow — Atoms give off extra energy as light

▲ WHY DO LUMINOUS PAINTS GLOW IN THE DARK?

Luminous paints glow in the dark. This is because they absorb light energy when they are in the light. As soon as it is dark, they **give out this energy as a bright glow. The glow fades when all the energy stored in the paint is used up.**

When any material is lit, the atoms in its molecules gain energy. But they lose this extra energy immediately by reflecting the light back. Luminous materials do not reflect all the light energy right away. They keep some energy and lose it gradually. This extra energy shows up as a glow in the dark.

Some materials seem to glow brightly in daylight. This is because they gain energy from the daylight like luminous paint, but immediately give off all the extra energy as light of one color. This is why the color looks bright. These materials are called fluorescent.

▶ HOW ARE STATUES MADE?

A sculptor may carve a statue from a block of stone or of wood. Using a hammer and chisel, he or she chips away at the block to form the statue. Metal statues are first made in clay, and a mold is made. The statue is cast by pouring molten metal into the mold and leaving it to set.

A sculptor who carves a statue has to take great care not to cut away too much stone or wood from the block. Then the final statue may be delicately polished to make the surface smooth and shiny.

Making a metal statue can be easier because the sculptor first works in clay. Instead of cutting away, he or she builds up the statue in clay. The figure can then be altered by taking some of the clay away or adding more. To support the clay figure, the sculptor builds it on a frame. The clay figure is then used to make a mold to produce the metal statue.

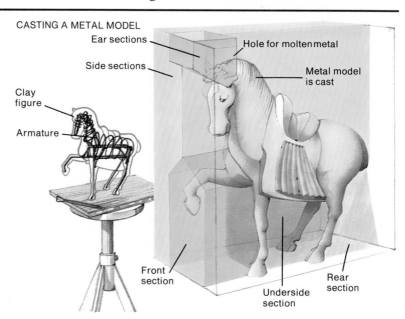

CASTING A METAL MODEL — Ear sections — Side sections — Clay figure — Armature — Hole for molten metal — Metal model is cast — Front section — Underside section — Rear section

▲ HOW ARE STATUES AND MODELS CAST?

First a clay figure is made, then a mold is made by covering the figure in plaster. The figure is removed, and the middle of the plaster mold is almost filled with a core of material. Then molten metal is poured between the mold and the core.

The "lost-wax" process is often used to cast metal statues. Hot wax is poured into a plaster mold of the clay figure. It sets to form a hollow copy of the figure.

The wax copy is then placed in a casting box and surrounded inside and out with fine sand. The sand fits around the wax impression to form another mold. Then liquid metal is poured through a hole into the mold. It melts the wax, which runs out of the mold, and then sets to produce a hollow metal statue or model.

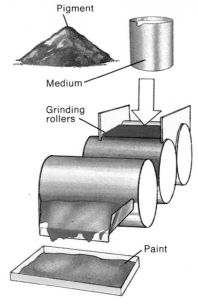

▲ HOW IS A MOSAIC MADE?

A mosaic is a picture or pattern made in a floor or on a wall. Thousands of tiny pieces of colored materials are fitted together. The design is worked out first, then the pieces are fixed in wet cement.

Mosaics are usually made with pieces of tile. The pieces are cut to the right size first and colored if necessary. Mosaics can also be made with glass, and small pebbles can be set in attractive patterns.

The design of the pattern or picture is first drawn on paper. Then it is scratched out in a layer of wet cement on the floor or wall. The pieces, which are called tesserae, are then fixed in place. When the cement is dry, the gaps between the tesserae are filled with a cement called grout.

To speed up this process, some mosaics are laid in sections made of tesserae fixed to a soft backing material.

▲ WHAT ARE PAINTS MADE OF?

Paints are made of colored powders called pigments and a liquid such as oil. The liquid sets hard when it is brushed onto a surface and colors it. Water colors are mixtures of pigments with a little water. The pigment stays on the paper when the water dries out.

Paints are made by grinding the pigments and a liquid medium between rollers. More of the medium and pigment may then be added to give the paint the right thickness and depth of color.

Oil paints and paints that protect surfaces often contain varnish as the medium. The varnish may come from natural oils or synthetic resins made like plastics.

Other paints contain solvents that evaporate, leaving the pigment in a film of resin. Emulsion paints contain synthetic resins that mix with water. As the paint dries, it leaves the resin behind on the surface.

▼ WHAT IS AN ETCHING?

An etching is a print made from a metal plate. The picture is drawn on a metal plate. Ink is applied to the plate and paper is rolled over it to make a print.

The etching plate is coated with a layer of a special varnish. Then the artist uses an etching tool with a sharp point to draw the picture on the plate. The point scrapes away the varnish, exposing the metal beneath.

Next, the plate is put into a bath of acid. The layer of varnish protects the plate, except where the tool has removed the coating. There it eats away the metal and forms grooves in the plate. On inking the plate, ink is left in the grooves. As the paper is rolled over the plate, it lifts the ink to print the picture.

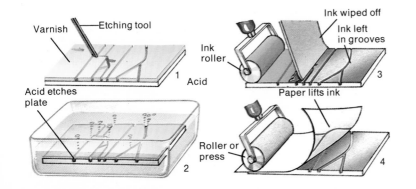

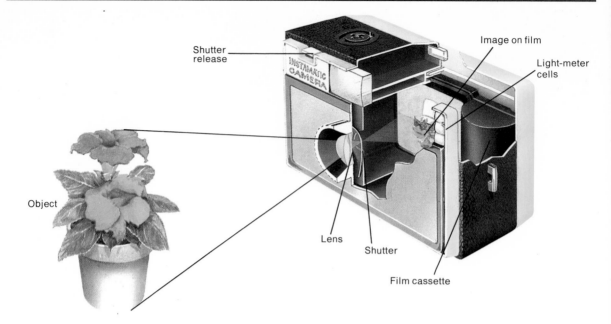

Shutter release

Image on film

Light-meter cells

Object

Lens

Shutter

Film cassette

▲ HOW DOES PHOTOGRAPHY WORK?

When you take a photo-graph, light enters the camera and makes a picture on the film. The light changes the film so that the picture shows up when the film is developed. This is done by placing the film in chemicals known as developers.

Black-and-white films contain a layer of a compound of silver. Color films have several layers. Where light strikes the silver compound, it partly changes it to silver. When the film is developed, the parts exposed to light are completely changed to silver. The parts that were not exposed still contain silver compound, which is removed. The silver forms a thin black layer in the film, giving a negative image of the picture. In this, the light parts are dark and the dark parts are light. A print, in which the dark parts are dark and the light parts are light, is then made from the negative.

▲ HOW DOES A CAMERA TAKE PICTURES?

The lens on the front of a camera makes a picture appear on the film inside the camera. By looking into the viewfinder, you can see the picture that the camera will take. You then press the shutter release to take the photo.

The light rays that come from an object in front of the camera are refracted (bent) by the lens to project an image of the object on to the film. The image is upside down and back to front, but the picture is seen the right way when a print or slide is made. When the shutter release is pressed, the shutter opens for a fraction of a second and exposes the film. The exposure is so short that moving objects appear to be still.

The lens may also have an aperture that opens or closes to let more or less light through the lens. The aperture is opened if the scene being photographed is not brightly lit.

▲ HOW DOES A LIGHT METER WORK?

A light meter tells you the brightness of the scene being photographed. Light from the scene goes into the light meter. It is then changed to a small electric current. This works a dial that shows you how to set the camera's shutter speed and aperture to take a good photograph.

A light meter contains light-sensitive cells that convert light rays into electricity. Alternatively, the cells change the strength of an electric current flowing through the cells from a small battery in the camera. Either way, a stronger electric current is produced when more light enters the meter. The current moves a needle so that you can check the brightness of the scene being photo-graphed.

From the position of the needle, you can see how to set the shutter and the aperture in order to make the correct exposure and get a good photograph.

► HOW DOES A FLASH WORK?

The bulbs in a flashcube contain metal wire or foil and a small tube of powder. When the shutter release is pressed, it makes a spring strike the tube and fire the powder. This heats the wire or foil in the bulb, making it burn brightly and produce a flash of light.

A flashbulb contains oxygen, so that the wire or foil burns with a very bright light. The light is slightly yellow and this is why flashbulbs for daylight color film are blue. The blue container changes the color of the flash to the white color of sunlight.

Some flashbulbs are fired by electricity. A switch inside the camera makes the bulb flash at exactly the same moment as the shutter opens. It does this by connecting a battery to the flashbulb.

Unlike a flashbulb, an electronic flash can be used again and again. The flash contains a tube that gives out a bright flash of white light when a strong electric charge passes through it.

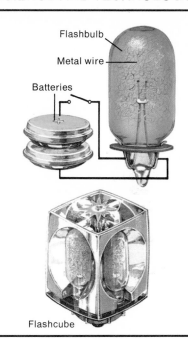

Flashbulb
Metal wire
Batteries

Flashcube

▼ HOW ARE COLOR SLIDES MADE?

A color film has three layers that take yellow, red and blue pictures of a scene. A color slide or print contains three layers that are yellow, red and blue. When you look at a color print or slides, these three colors combine in various ways to give a full-color picture.

A color film is made of three layers of light-sensitive emulsion containing silver compounds. The three layers are sensitive to different colors in the light. The film also contains a transparent yellow band which helps to separate the colors in the light. When a color film is developed to make a color slide, as shown here, the silver produced in the exposed parts of the three layers is replaced by yellow, red and blue dyes, and the yellow band is removed. When the slide is viewed, white light passes through it to the eyes. The yellow, red and blue images combine to give a full-color picture. For example, the yellow and blue layers combine to give green. Black is given by all three layers, and white is seen if all the layers are clear. A color print also contains three layers of yellow, red and blue, like a color slide.

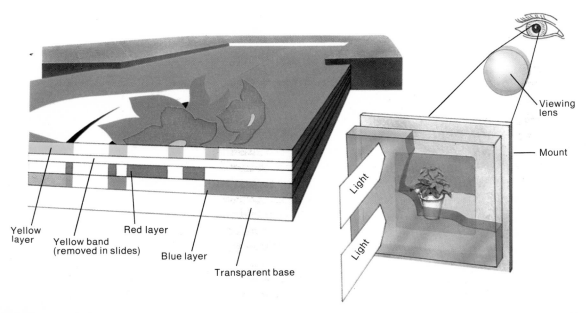

Yellow layer
Yellow band (removed in slides)
Red layer
Blue layer
Transparent base

Viewing lens
Mount
Light
Light

▼ HOW DOES A FILM PROJECTOR WORK?

A film is a long strip of still pictures. As it passes through the projector, each picture is lit up and a lens projects an image of the picture on the screen. The pictures are projected so quickly that they appear to be moving.

A cinema film is projected at a rate of 24 frames (still pictures) per second. Home projectors are slower. The film has a row of sprocket holes along one or both edges. Sprockets in the projector pull the film into the film gate. The film then stops for a moment and light from a lamp passes through the frame. The lens projects the picture on the screen. The sprockets then turn and advance the film to show the next frame. As the film moves, the blade of a rotating shutter passes between the lamp and the film so that the movement of the film does not show on the screen.

In sound films, light from the lamp passes through the sound track and strikes a light-sensitive cell, which produces an electric signal. The signal varies in strength as the sound track passes. It goes to an amplifier and loud-speaker, which gives the sound.

In some sound films, the sound is recorded on a magnetic strip along the film like a tape recording.

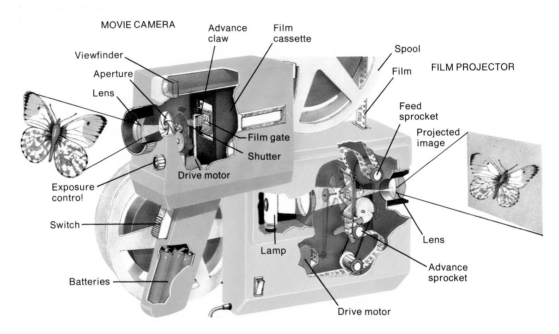

MOVIE CAMERA — Advance claw — Film cassette — Viewfinder — Aperture — Lens — Film gate — Shutter — Drive motor — Exposure control — Switch — Batteries — Lamp — Spool — Film — FILM PROJECTOR — Feed sprocket — Projected image — Lens — Advance sprocket — Drive motor

▲ HOW DOES A MOVIE CAMERA WORK?

A movie camera has a film like an ordinary camera. But instead of taking just one picture at a time, it takes many pictures every second. As the film moves past the lens in the camera, a shutter continually opens and closes to give a long line of pictures on the film. Then the film is developed and shown on a screen.

Many movie cameras take a cassette of film. The cassette contains a long strip of film that lasts several minutes. It has an opening through which the film passes into the film gate. A claw mechanism pulls on the sprocket holes in the film to advance it frame by frame. The film stops in the film gate as the claw moves back, and the shutter opens briefly to expose the film. The aperture of the lens may be set by an automatic exposure control. The shutter then closes as the claw advances the film.

In many movie cameras, the shutter consists of a rotating half disk. To make slow-motion films, the speed of the film is increased so that more frames are exposed every second. However, the projector always runs at the same speed. The film takes longer to pass through the projector than the camera, which slows down the action. Slowing the camera speed down speeds up the action.

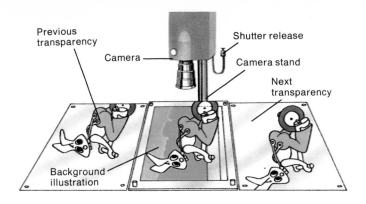

Previous transparency
Camera
Shutter release
Camera stand
Next transparency
Background illustration

▲ HOW ARE CARTOON FILMS MADE?

In a cartoon film, drawings seem to move. In fact you are seeing 24 different drawings every second, which gives the illusion of movement. Each of the drawings is photographed separately with a special movie camera.

Each frame of the cartoon is photographed on an animation stand. The drawing is placed on a table and the camera is mounted on a frame above. So that artists need not paint the whole of every frame, parts of the picture are painted on separate transparent sheets. Then these are placed on top of a background illustration to build up each frame.

Cartoon makers also use computers to produce the drawings. The artist draws on an electronic board with a special pen. The computer then fills in the color.

▶ HOW DOES A MICROPHONE WORK?

Sound waves make a microphone produce an electric signal. This signal goes to an amplifier and loudspeaker.

Inside the microphone, the sound waves strike a thin plate called a diaphragm. The diaphragm vibrates at the same rate as the sound waves. It is connected to a device that produces an electric signal varying in strength at the same rate as the vibrations.

In a crystal microphone, a piezoelectric crystal generates the signal by responding to pressure placed on it by the diaphragm. Moving-coil microphones contain small coils of wire suspended between the poles of a magnet. The diaphragm vibrates the coils to give a signal.

Ribbon microphones are similar but have a metal ribbon instead of coils. Condenser and carbon microphones are fed with an electric current, and vibration of a condenser or carbon granules varies the current to create a signal.

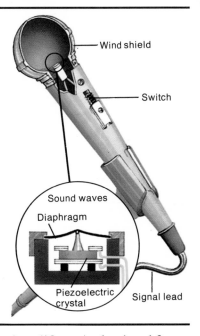

Wind shield
Switch
Sound waves
Diaphragm
Piezoelectric crystal
Signal lead

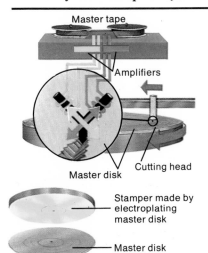

Master tape
Amplifiers
Master disk
Cutting head
Stamper made by electroplating master disk
Master disk

◀ HOW ARE RECORDS MADE?

Most records are first recorded on tape in a recording studio and a master disk is made from the tape. Molds called stampers are then made from the master disk. The records are produced by pressing a piece of plastic between the stampers.

The master tape made in the studio has two sound tracks.

Amplifiers send a signal from each track to the cutting head of a disk cutter. The head cuts a groove in the lacquer coating of a master disk by using the two signals to form the walls of the groove. A stamper is then made by electroplating the master disk and peeling away the layer of metal formed. This has ridges where the record has grooves.

To manufacture the final record, a piece of plastic is pressed between two stampers.

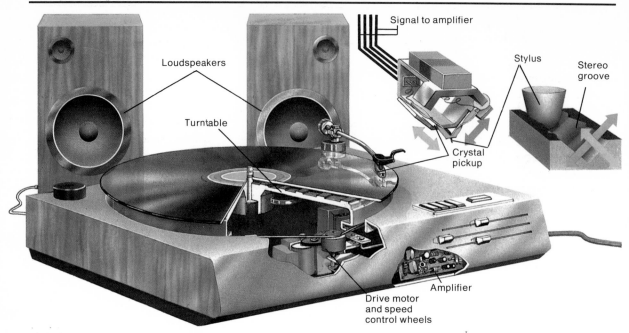

Labels on diagram: Loudspeakers · Signal to amplifier · Stylus · Stereo groove · Turntable · Crystal pickup · Drive motor and speed control wheels · Amplifier

▲ HOW DOES A RECORD PLAYER WORK?

When you play a record, you place the needle on the pickup of the record player in the groove of the record. As the record turns, the tiny curves in the groove make the needle vibrate. This causes the pickup to produce an electric signal. The signal goes to an amplifier and a loudspeaker to give the music.

There are two kinds of pickups for record players. Crystal pickups contain a piezoelectric crystal. The crystal is connected to the needle, or stylus. As the stylus vibrates in the groove, it continually twists the crystal, making it produce an electric signal.

Magnetic pickups contain tiny coils of wire that vibrate between the poles of magnets and generate a signal. Some record players contain an amplifier and a loudspeaker. With others, these have to be connected to the record player.

▲ HOW DOES A LOUDSPEAKER PRODUCE SOUNDS?

A loudspeaker makes the sounds that come from record and cassette players, radio and television sets. Inside the loudspeaker is a cone of a material such as plastic. It is connected to a coil or wire and a magnet. When an electric signal is fed to the loudspeaker, the magnet makes the coil move. The cone vibrates and the sound comes out.

When the electric signal is fed to the coil, it produces a varying magnetic field. A magnet placed around it attracts and repels the coil, which in turn vibrates the loudspeaker cone. The cone and its coil and magnet are known as a drive unit. Many loudspeakers have several drive units. Large units produce deep sounds and small units give high sounds.

In an electrostatic loudspeaker a plate is made to vibrate by electrostatic forces and not by magnetic fields.

▲ HOW DOES STEREO WORK?

When you hear a stereo record or cassette, the sound comes from two loudspeakers. The sounds appear to be spread out between them. This is because the music is recorded on the tape or record in two parts called tracks. One goes to the left-hand speaker and the other to the right-hand speaker.

When the master tape is made in the studio, the sound is recorded in two tracks along the tape. One is a left-hand track and the other a right-hand track. The sounds are divided between the two tracks. An instrument that is only on the left-hand track comes from the left-hand speaker, while a singer recorded on both tracks comes from both speakers.

On a record, the two tracks are recorded in the two walls of the groove. The pickup has two crystals or coils that produce two signals which go to the loudspeakers.

▼ HOW DOES A TAPE RECORDER WORK?

A tape recorder works by changing sound waves into magnetism. The sound is recorded as a magnetic pattern along the recording tape. When the tape is played, the magnetic pattern is turned back into sound.

A microphone is usually connected to the tape recorder, although many cassette recorders contain their own microphone. It turns the sound into an electric signal, which is amplified by the recorder's amplifier and then fed to the record head. The head is a coil of wire wound around an iron ring with a gap in it. The signal causes the head to produce a varying magnetic field. As the tape passes the head, it is magnetized by it. To play the tape, it is moved over the head again and the passing magnetic field makes the coil give out an electric signal. The signal then goes to an amplifier and loudspeaker connected to the head.

In many recorders, the same head is used to record and to play tapes. High-quality machines have separate heads for record and playback. When a tape is being recorded, another head erases any recording that is already on the tape. It produces a magnetic field that removes any magnetism from the tape.

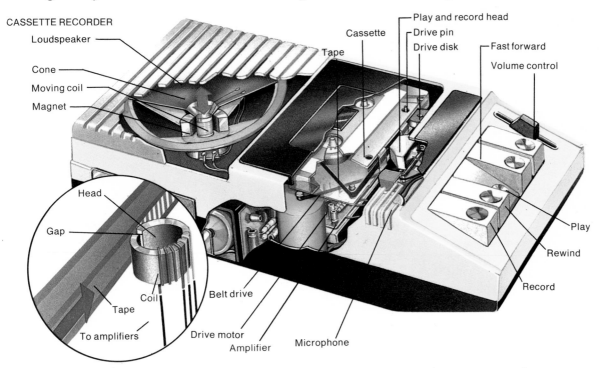

CASSETTE RECORDER
Loudspeaker
Cone
Moving coil
Magnet
Cassette
Tape
Play and record head
Drive pin
Drive disk
Fast forward
Volume control
Play
Rewind
Record
Head
Gap
Coil
Tape
To amplifiers
Belt drive
Drive motor
Amplifier
Microphone

▲ HOW ARE CASSETTES MADE?

Like a record, music cassettes are produced from a master tape made in a recording studio. It is played back very fast and the speeded-up sounds are recorded on tape also traveling at a high speed. This tape is then used to make cassettes.

Recording tape at high speed enables copies of tapes to be made very quickly. Both the copy of the master tape and the tape used to make the cassettes are speeded up by the same amount. Then when the cassette tape is played at its normal speed, the original music will be heard.

A cassette has two sides. The music of one side is recorded along the top of the tape, and the other side is recorded along the bottom. The head of the cassette player lines up with the top of the tape. To hear the other side, the cassette is turned over.

Both sides of the cassette are recorded at once. The copy of the master tape used to make cassettes has both sides recorded on it: one playing forwards and one playing backwards. When the cassette is turned over to play the other side, the music comes out forwards.

As a cassette is put into a player, the centers of the reels fit over spindles that turn the reels.

▲ HOW DOES CITIZEN'S BAND RADIO WORK?

You can talk on the radio by using the citizen's band radio. You have a small radio set that is both a transmitter and a receiver. As you speak, the set sends out radio waves over a few miles. Anyone receiving your transmission can listen and then reply. You then receive the radio waves that they transmit.

To prevent radio stations from interfering with each other, each one is allocated a different frequency for transmission. The frequencies are grouped in bands, each of which has a different kind of use.

In many countries, the citizen's band is allocated for private use. The sets operate on several channels within the band, and the signals are weak so that they do not carry very far. In this way, many people can use the citizen's band without interfering with one another. Citizen's band radio is popular with car and truck drivers.

▼ HOW FAR CAN RADIO TRAVEL?

The radio waves that carry television pictures move in a straight line from the transmitter to the antenna. They can go only as far as the distance from the transmitter to the horizon. Waves carrying radio broadcasts can move over the horizon. Some radio transmissions can travel around the world.

Low-frequency (long-wave) radio waves can travel over the horizon and pass around mountains. Depending on their power, these signals can cross continents and oceans.

High-frequency (short-wave) signals do not bend in this way. They travel in straight lines, but are reflected back to Earth from the upper atmosphere. In this way, they can bounce around the world. Television signals are sent to communications satellites in orbit. They cut through the atmosphere, and the satellite transmits them back to the Earth below. Out in space, radio signals can travel very long distances.

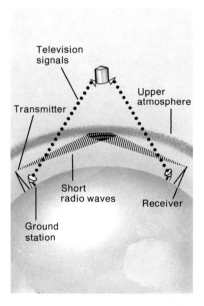

Television signals

Transmitter

Upper atmosphere

Short radio waves

Receiver

Ground station

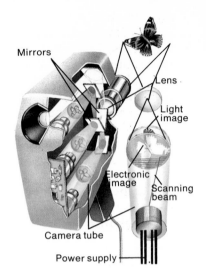

Mirrors

Lens

Light image

Electronic image

Scanning beam

Camera tube

Power supply

▲ HOW DOES A TELEVISION CAMERA WORK?

A television camera produces an image on a light-sensitive tube. This tube turns the light in the image into an electric signal. When the signal goes to a television set, the picture appears on the screen.

The lens of a television camera projects an image of the scene before it into the camera tube. In color television cameras, there are three tubes that respond to the red, blue and green light in the image.

Colored mirrors or prisms split the image into three colors. Each image falls on a light-sensitive plate, producing a pattern of electrons that form an electronic image on a target behind the plate. A beam of electrons scans the target in a sequence of lines. The intensity of the electron image makes the beam vary in strength. It produces a vision signal that varies according to the brightness of each part of the image that is scanned.

▼ HOW DOES RADIO WORK?

When you switch on a radio, it picks up invisible radio waves. The waves come through the air from a transmitter. At the radio station, music or speech is changed into an electric signal. This signal goes to the transmitter and is changed into radio waves. The antenna of your radio picks up the radio waves. The radio changes the waves back into sound.

The transmitter of a radio station sends out a carrier wave at a particular frequency. The frequency is measured in hertz (Hz). The carrier wave is produced by sending an electric signal that alternates at this frequency to the transmitter. The frequency is so rapid that it causes electrons in the metal atoms of the transmitter to vibrate and give out radio waves at the frequency.

However, the carrier signal is first combined with a sound signal from the microphones at the radio station's studio. This causes the carrier wave to vary in such a way that it carries the sound as variations in its strength or frequency. The carrier wave strikes the radio antenna and loosens the electrons in its atoms to produce a weak electric signal at the same frequency.

The tuner in the radio detects this frequency, and removes the carrier signal to give the sound signal.

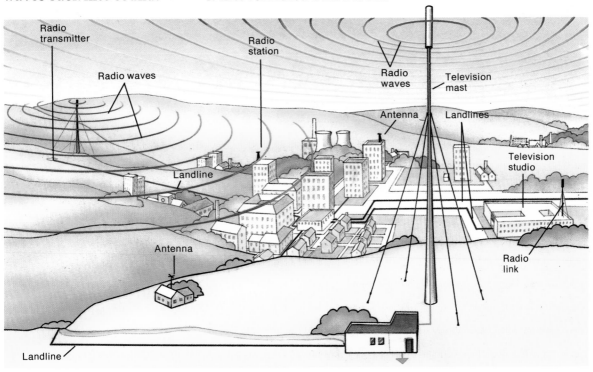

▲ HOW DO TELEVISION PICTURES GET TO HOMES?

At the television studio, the cameras produce electric signals. These picture signals then go to the television transmitter near your home. The transmitter turns the signals into radio waves that spread out through the air. The antenna on your set picks up the waves, and the television set turns them back into pictures.

The signals from the studio usually travel along cables called landlines to the transmitter. Radio links may also be used to send the signals to distant transmitters.

Large television masts serve big cities. However, the radio waves that carry the picture signals do not travel very far. Country areas are therefore served by local repeater transmitters. Each home usually has its own antenna on or inside the roof, or on the set.

The pictures and the sound of a television transmission are carried by a carrier wave in the same way as radio. Television programs can even be transmitted from satellites in space to homes. Large dish-shaped antennas are needed to pick up the transmissions. Television also reaches many homes by cable. In this case, the sound and picture signals are not transmitted by radio, but are sent through a cable directly to homes.

55

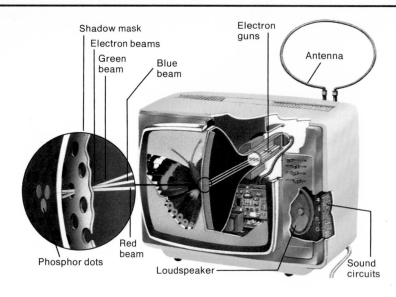

Shadow mask
Electron beams
Green beam
Blue beam
Electron guns
Antenna
Phosphor dots
Red beam
Loudspeaker
Sound circuits

◀ HOW DOES COLOR TELEVISION WORK?

If you look closely at a color television picture, you will see that it is made up of tiny red, green and blue dots or stripes. These three colors mix together when you look at the screen from a distance to give a full-color picture.

A color camera produces three vision signals corresponding to the red, green and blue light in the scene. A color set receives these three signals and sends them to three electron guns. Three electron beams scan the screen, one for each color.

The whole screen is made up of a mosaic of dots or stripes of phosphor that glow red, green and blue when struck by the electron beams. To make sure that each beam produces the right color, the beams pass through holes in a shadow mask behind the screen. The angles of the beams and the holes are arranged so that each beam can only pass through to strike phosphors of the correct color.

▲ HOW DOES A TELEVISION SET WORK?

The television antenna picks up a signal from the transmitter. The signal goes to the tube in the set. Inside the tube, a beam of electrons (tiny electric particles) is fired in lines across the screen. The screen lights up in lines that make up a picture.

The signal received by the antenna is a copy of the vision signal produced by the camera. This signal goes to

the controls of an electron gun that fires a beam of electrons at the screen. Where the beam strikes the back of the screen, it produces a dot of light.

The beam scans the screen in the same sequence of lines as in the camera, and builds up a picture on the screen. A new picture is produced 25 or 30 times a second, so that the image appears to move. The sound is produced in the same way as in a radio set.

▶ HOW DOES A VIDEO RECORDER WORK?

You can record a television program on a video cassette using a video recorder. The video cassette contains tape like a tape cassette. It records the electric signal coming from the antenna.

A video recorder records vision or video signals as magnetic patterns in a track along the tape. It has record and replay heads similar to those in sound tape recorders,

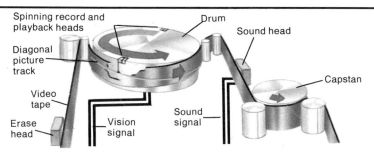

Spinning record and playback heads
Drum
Sound head
Diagonal picture track
Video tape
Erase head
Vision signal
Sound signal
Capstan

but the tape has to move much faster over the head than with sound recording.

In fact, the tape does not move quickly; instead, the head does. There are two heads mounted in a rotating drum, around which the tape

moves. The heads spin rapidly as the drum passes along the tape, recording the vision signal in a series of diagonal tracks across the tape. The sound is recorded in a straight track along one edge of the tape.

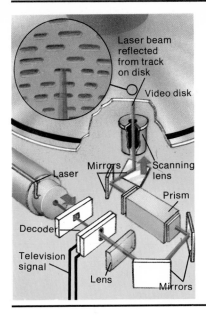

Laser beam reflected from track on disk

Video disk

Mirrors

Scanning lens

Laser

Prism

Decoder

Television signal

Lens

Mirrors

◀ WHAT IS A VIDEO DISK?

A video disk is like a phonograph record except that it has pictures recorded on it as well as sound. To see the film on the disk, you play it on a video disk player connected to a television set.

You cannot make your own video recordings on a video disk player. You can only play what is recorded on the disk.

There are several different video disk systems. One has a spiral groove in the record and a pickup with a stylus that rests in the groove. The picture signal is recorded as a sequence of electric charges that is detected by an electrode in the stylus.

A similar system does away with the groove by guiding an electrode over a spiral track of pits stamped in the surface of the disk.

A third system, shown here, uses a laser beam to scan a spiral track. As the record spins, the reflected beam varies in intensity and goes to a decoder that produces the vision signal.

▶ HOW DOES AN AQUALUNG WORK?

An aqualung is used by a diver to swim freely underwater. The diver carries a cylinder of compressed air on his or her back. Air from the cylinder goes to a mouthpiece. This allows the diver to breathe air in from the cylinder.

For the diver to be able to breathe easily, the pressure of the air must be equal to the pressure of the water around the diver. A flexible diaphragm moves in and out to regulate the air pressure as the diver breathes.

On breathing in, the air pressure in the mouthpiece falls slightly and water pressure forces the diaphragm inwards. The diaphragm operates a lever to open the inlet valve on the air hose connected to the cylinder and air flows to the diver.

On breathing out, the air pressure moves the diaphragm back, cutting off the air supply. Valves open to let this air escape.

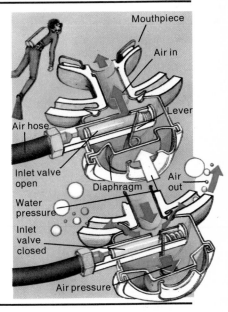

Mouthpiece

Air in

Lever

Air hose

Inlet valve open

Diaphragm

Air out

Water pressure

Inlet valve closed

Air pressure

◀ HOW DOES A PARACHUTE WORK?

When a parachute opens, it billows out above the parachutist. The large canopy of the parachute pulls against the air and slows the fall. The parachutist can pull on lines attached to the canopy to try and land in a particular place.

The parachute is packed carefully with a pilot chute that pulls out the main canopy. The canopy may have gaps that allow the air through in a controlled flow. The air resistance of the canopy cancels out the weight of the parachutist. The parachutist then falls at a constant speed and strikes the ground at about 13 feet per second. This is the same as jumping off a wall just over 4 feet high. As the parachutist lands, he or she pulls a quick-release catch. Some parachutes are shaped like squares and have lines of cells that blow out to form a simple wing. The parachutist has more control with this type.

▶ HOW DO MAGNETS WORK?

Inside a magnet are lots of very tiny magnets. These are not separate objects, but very small parts of the magnet that each act like a tiny magnet. In a magnet, these tiny magnetic parts line up in rows.

The magnetic parts are called domains. An unmagnetized material contains domains, but their magnetism points in different directions, so that the magnetism of each domain is cancelled out by other domains, so the material has no overall magnetism.

But when a strong magnetic field is used to magnetize the material, it lines up the magnetism of each domain so that its magnetic effect acts in the same direction.

When a magnet is cut or broken, each piece is still magnetic because its domains are still lined up. The magnetism of the domains is caused by the electrons in the atoms of the material. They produce a magnetic effect as they spin around the nucleus (center) of each atom.

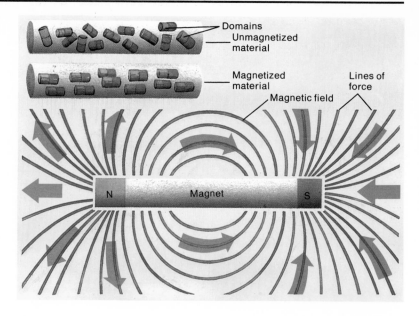

Domains
Unmagnetized material
Magnetized material
Lines of force
Magnetic field
N Magnet S

▲ WHAT IS A MAGNETIC FIELD?

Every magnet has a magnetic field. This is the invisible force that makes the magnet pick up steel pins and other objects. It also makes magnets pull or push on each other.

Every magnet has a north pole (N) and a south pole (S). You can find which pole is which by suspending a magnet from a string. It turns until the north pole faces north and the south pole faces south.

Invisible lines of magnetic force curve out between the two poles. These lines make up the magnetic field of the magnet. When two magnets approach, their magnetic fields act on each other. The magnets attract one another only if a north pole meets a south pole. If the two poles are the same, the magnets repel one another.

The Earth has a magnetic field that extends from the poles all over the globe. It causes a magnetic compass to turn and point towards the poles.

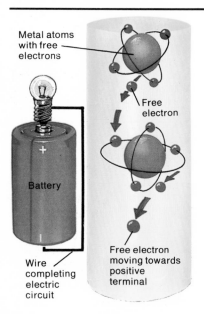

Metal atoms with free electrons
Free electron
Battery
Wire completing electric circuit
Free electron moving towards positive terminal

◀ HOW DOES ELECTRICITY FLOW ALONG A WIRE?

When electricity flows in a wire, tiny particles called electrons move through the wire. Each electron has a very small electric charge. As the electrons arrive, they produce electricity. To make a bulb in a room light up, about two million million million electrons flow every second.

The electrons come from a source of electricity like

batteries or the generators in power stations. Each electron has a negative electric charge. The electrons leave the negative terminal and flow through the wire to the positive terminal to complete an electric circuit.

Electricity only flows through metals like copper and steel. This is because the electrons in the outer part of the atoms of these metals are free to move. These free electrons drift from one metal atom to the next. This makes an electric charge flow rapidly along the wire.

▶ HOW DOES A CAR BATTERY WORK?

A car battery does not run out of electricity, since it can be recharged. The battery contains plates bathed in acid. The acid changes the material in the plates and makes them produce electricity. Feeding electricity back into the battery changes the plates back to the first material.

The plates of a car battery are arranged in pairs. One plate in each pair is made of spongy lead and the other is lead oxide. The pairs are suspended in dilute sulfuric acid. Separator plates keep them apart, and dividers group the plates into cells within the battery.

All the lead plates are connected together and to the negative terminal of the battery. The lead oxide plates are all wired up to the positive terminal. To produce current, the sulfuric acid attacks the plates. It changes both the lead and the lead oxide into lead sulfate. As it does so, electrons are produced at the lead plate and flow to the lead oxide plate, creating an electric current.

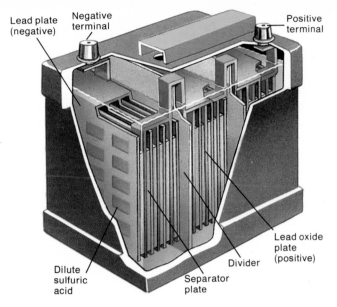

Lead plate (negative)
Negative terminal
Positive terminal
Dilute sulfuric acid
Separator plate
Divider
Lead oxide plate (positive)

▼ HOW DOES AN ELECTRIC MOTOR WORK?

When you switch on an electric motor, it makes something rotate. This could be the wheels of a toy train, for example. The electric current makes a wire coil inside the motor become magnetic. A magnet then makes the coil turn, and this powers a shaft.

The electric current flows from a battery through a coil suspended between the poles of a magnet. The coil produces a magnetic field whose poles move towards the poles of the magnet. The north pole of the coil is attracted towards the magnet's south pole. The south pole of the coil's field similarly moves towards the magnet's north pole. As a result, the coil rotates.

As its poles pass the magnet's poles, the electric current suddenly reverses and flows in the opposite direction. The commutator causes this to happen. As the current reverses, so does the coil's magnetic field. The south pole becomes a north pole and vice-versa, so that the coil is now repelled by the poles of the magnet to which it was previously attracted.

In this way, the coil keeps moving. The commutator reverses the current flow every half turn.

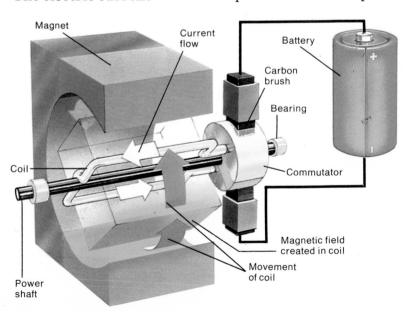

Magnet
Current flow
Battery
Carbon brush
Bearing
Coil
Commutator
Magnetic field created in coil
Movement of coil
Power shaft

▶ HOW DOES A TRANSFORMER WORK?

A transformer changes the voltage of an electric current. Inside the transformer, the current enters a coil and the coil produces a magnetic field. The field makes another current flow in another coil in the transformer.

A transformer increases or decreases the voltage of an alternating current. This kind of current reverses its direction of flow many times a second.

Transformers are used to produce electricity at very high voltage for long distance transmission. This voltage is then lowered in more transformers before reaching homes.

The current enters the

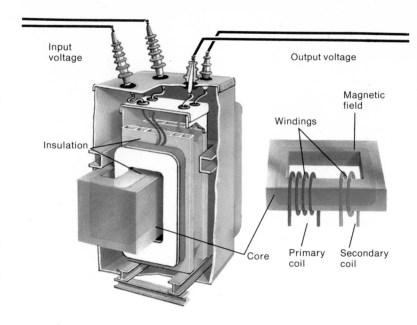

primary coil of the transformer, which generates a magnetic field in an iron core inside the coil. The field continually reverses as the current does so. It cuts

through a secondary coil around the core, producing another alternating current in the coil.

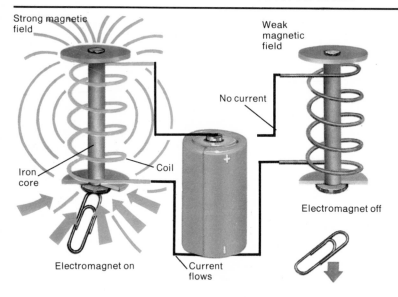

▲ HOW DOES AN ELECTROMAGNET WORK?

An electromagnet is a kind of magnet worked by electricity. Its magnetism can be switched on and off. It contains a coil of wire wound around an iron bar. When an electric current

flows through the coil, the bar becomes strongly magnetic.

The iron core inside the coil of an electromagnet produces a much stronger magnetic field than the coil alone. This is because the coil magnetizes the iron the instant that the

current is switched on. However, the iron core does not keep this magnetism when the electromagnet is switched off. It is demagnetized immediately.

Large electromagnets on cranes are used to raise and transport loads of scrap iron. The electromagnet picks up the iron when it is switched on, and the crane moves it to the required place. Then the current is switched off and the scrap iron falls to the ground.

Electromagnets are used to produce strong magnetic fields in many electrical machines, including electric motors and generators. They can also produce varying magnetic fields, depending on the strength of the current fed to them. Electromagnets are therefore used in making electrical meters to measure things, and in tape recorders and loudspeakers.

▼ WHAT DOES A TRANSISTOR DO?

Electrical machines like radio and television sets contain transistors. The transistors increase small electric currents. They can also switch the currents on or off.

A transistor is made up of three layers of a material called a semiconductor. The thin central layer is called the base, and the two thick outer layers are the emitter and the collector.

A current flows from the emitter to the collector, but is stopped by the base. A low electric signal is fed to the base to alter its electrical nature. If this signal increases, the base lets through more current. If it decreases, the base restricts the flow of current.

The flow of current through the transistor therefore varies in the same way as the base signal fed to the transistor. As the current is greater than the signal, the transistor amplifies the signal. If the base signal is zero, no current flows through the transistor.

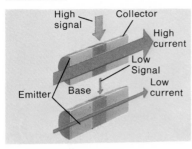

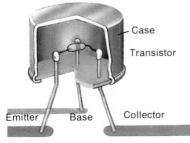

▲ HOW CAN MICROCHIPS BE SO SMALL?

Inside an electronic machine, such as a calculator, are microchips containing many thousands of parts like transistors. Because there are so many parts, they have to be small. The electrons that make up the current are very tiny, so the parts can be made very small too.

A tiny microchip may contain hundreds of thousands of transistors and other electronic components. This great number is necessary because the microchip has to carry out very many electronic operations very quickly to do calculations. If the parts are small and close together, the electric currents can flow between the various components very rapidly.

As all the components can be made of silicon, they are manufactured as small as possible inside a single chip of silicon – the microchip.

▲ HOW ARE MICROCHIPS MADE?

Microchips are made from very thin slices of a material called silicon. The tiny electronic parts inside the microchip are formed on the surface of a slice. Several layers of silicon are added in tiny but very complicated patterns.

Each layer of components is formed on the surface of the silicon by etching. A pattern outlining the shapes of the components is reduced by a photographic method and projected on the surface. It produces a mask with holes in the shape of the pattern.

The silicon is then treated with materials that penetrate the holes in the mask and alter the electrical nature of the silicon beneath. In this way, the surface is covered with a layer of tiny regions having different electrical properties.

This process is repeated several times, forming the components of the chip and their connections.

► **HOW DOES A DIGITAL WATCH WORK?**

A digital watch shows the time in numbers. At the heart of the watch is a quartz crystal which vibrates an exact number of times every second. Every time it vibrates, it produces an electric signal. The other parts of the watch count the signals and change the numbers in the display to show the right time.

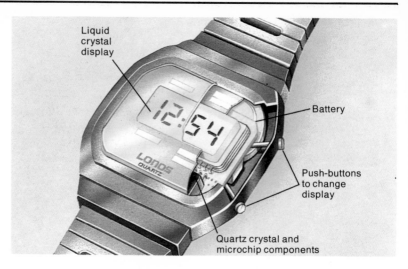

Liquid crystal display

Battery

Push-buttons to change display

Quartz crystal and microchip components

The quartz crystal gives out an electric signal when it is stretched or compressed. An electric current is fed from the batteries in the watch to make the crystal vibrate at an exact frequency.

The quartz crystal gives out an electric signal at this frequency, and it goes to the microchip components in the watch. These count the signals produced by the quartz crystal, and every second send another signal to the digital display to change the time that is shown.

The microchip can also count up the seconds to display minutes and hours and to show the date, even working out the change from one month to the next.

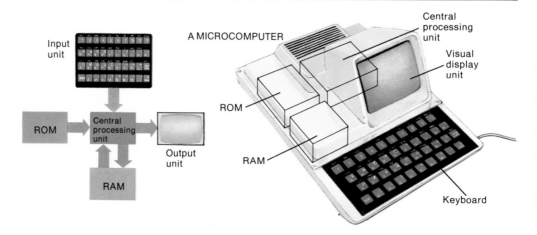

Input unit

A MICROCOMPUTER

Central processing unit

Visual display unit

ROM

ROM

Central processing unit

Output unit

RAM

RAM

Keyboard

▲ **HOW DOES A COMPUTER OPERATE?**

To make a computer work, you have to give it a program. This tells the computer what to do to perform a particular task, like adding up. Then you give it information (data) such as numbers that it needs to start, and the computer works out the answer.

Every computer, no matter how large or small, contains four basic units. These are the input, memory, central processing and output units.

The input unit is often a keyboard. It is used to feed a new program of instructions into the computer, and also data or information such as numbers. Both the program and data are held in a part of the memory unit called the RAM. They may also be fed to the RAM from a magnetic tape or disk that stores programs and data.

Another part of the memory unit called the ROM contains instructions that operate the central processing unit. This unit then follows the program and works out results from the data.

Finally, the central processor sends the results to the output unit, which may be a screen or printer.

Binary	Decimal
∅ ∅ ∅ ∅	0
∅ ∅ ∅ 1	1
∅ ∅ 1 ∅	2
∅ ∅ 1 1	3
∅ 1 ∅ ∅	4
∅ 1 ∅ 1	5
∅ 1 1 ∅	6
∅ 1 1 1	7
1 ∅ ∅ ∅	8

▲ HOW MANY NUMBERS DO COMPUTERS USE?

Computers work by using only two numbers – 0 and 1. A computer changes numbers and words into codes made up of 0s and 1s. It makes calculations with these codes.

The codes of 0s and 1s used by computers are known as binary numbers. All the program instructions and the data are fed into computers in the form of decimal numbers, letters, symbols and signs. Each of these has a particular binary number that is produced by the input unit. They consist not of figures, but of electric pulses.

When a pulse arrives at any point in the computer, it represents a 1. If no pulse arrives, there is a 0. The codes are stored in the computer's memory as on-off sequences of electric charge or magnetism.

The central processor calculates by combining the pulse sequences in various ways, producing a binary number that is decoded to give the result.

▼ HOW FAST DO COMPUTERS WORK?

The most powerful super-computers can do about 100 million calculations every second! However, each one is a simple piece of arithmetic, like adding two numbers together. The computer splits up a difficult problem into many of these simple pieces of arithmetic.

One of the most difficult problems is forecasting the weather. To work out how the atmosphere is going to behave tomorrow takes many millions of calculations. Only a supercomputer can do this before the weather actually happens.

A computer can work this fast because it breaks all its calculations down into codes of electric signals. The electric pulses that make up the codes move through the tiny circuits in the computer's microchips in extremely short times. The computer's central processor arranges the pulses to form new codes and carry out the calculations millions of times a second.

▼ HOW ARE COMPUTERS ABLE TO SPEAK?

Some computers can speak to people. They have a voice unit that can produce a certain number of words. Each word has its own electric code. A microchip in the computer produces the codes which go to the voice unit.

The voice unit of a computer contains a voice synthesizer. To get the words into the synthesizer, a person speaks the words into a machine that converts the sounds into digital signals. These are sequences of electric pulses like the binary codes that make computers work. The signals are then stored in the synthesizer's memory unit.

When the computer speaks, it takes the codes of the words required from the memory. It then changes the codes into electric signals that go to an amplifier and loudspeaker to produce the words.

Speaking computers are used to give information to people. They can also read books to blind people.

▼ HOW DOES A NUCLEAR REACTOR WORK?

Nuclear power stations contain nuclear reactors which use uranium fuel. The uranium gets very hot and a coolant (a liquid or gas) moves through the reactor to be heated. Then the hot coolant goes to a boiler to make steam, which powers electricity generators.

Inside the fuel rods in the reactor core, uranium nuclei split as neutron particles strike them. The smaller nuclei and other particles produced move off at great speed, producing heat. To prevent this chain reaction speeding up so that all the uranium atoms split too quickly, control rods are lowered into the reactor. They soak up neutrons so that the rate of splitting slows. If the reactor begins to overheat, the control rods automatically drop into the reactor to stop it working.

The coolant is usually water or carbon dioxide gas. It passes through a heat exchanger in the boiler, making water flowing around the heat exchanger boil. In some nuclear reactors, the reactor boils water to steam directly in the core. The steam is then piped to steam turbines, which in turn drive electricity generators. The steam is condensed back into water, which returns to the boiler or reactor.

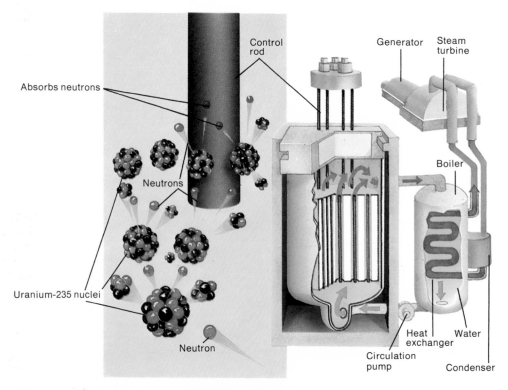

Control rod

Generator   Steam turbine

Absorbs neutrons

Neutrons

Boiler

Uranium-235 nuclei

Neutron

Heat exchanger   Water

Circulation pump   Condenser

▲ WHY IS NUCLEAR ENERGY SO POWERFUL?

Nuclear energy is produced by the tiny particles in the nuclei (centers) of atoms. These particles are held together by very strong forces. Breaking the nuclei releases these forces, giving great power.

In a reactor, a nuclear reaction is controlled to give useful energy. The nuclear fuel is a rare form of uranium metal called uranium-235.

When the nucleus of a uranium-235 atom is struck by a neutron, it breaks into two smaller nuclei and several more neutrons. These neutrons may then strike other uranium nuclei, causing them to split and give out yet more neutrons. In this way, more and more uranium nuclei split.

The reactor's control rods absorb most of the extra neutrons produced to keep the nuclear reaction going at a steady rate. As the nuclei split apart, the very strong forces holding the nuclear particles together are released. They make the neutrons and smaller nuclei move at immense speed, producing great heat. In this way, some of the mass of the uranium is turned into energy. Conversion of a little mass produces a lot of energy.

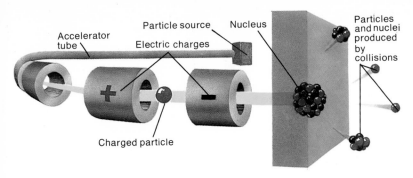

Accelerator tube
Particle source
Electric charges
Nucleus
Charged particle
Particles and nuclei produced by collisions

▲ HOW CAN ATOMS BE SPLIT?

Everything is made of tiny particles called atoms which cannot be broken apart. If they could, everything would fall apart.

However, scientists can split atoms to find out about the particles inside them.

Scientists split atoms in large machines called particle accelerators. These machines

use powerful electric charges to send a beam of particles along a tube. These are particles like protons that have an electric charge. The charges on the tube push or pull the particles, accelerating them to a very high speed.

The beam is then directed to a target. The particles collide with atoms in the target and split the nucleus in some of the atoms. The nucleus breaks into more particles and smaller nuclei, which move into a detector. The detector identifies the particles coming from the broken nucleus.

▶ HOW DO WE KNOW HOW OLD FOSSILS ARE?

Fossils are the remains of prehistoric animals and plants. They are thousands or millions of years old. A fossil, or the rock in which it is found, is very slightly radioactive. Scientists can tell how old fossils are by measuring this radioactivity.

Over a certain time, the radioactivity of a material decreases steadily to zero. It may take thousands or millions of years

for a material to lose its radioactivity.

Plants and animals contain very small amounts of radioactive elements. Their radioactivity begins to decrease as soon as they die. Measuring this radioactivity therefore gives their age.

Radioactive minerals in rocks begin to lose their radioactivity as soon as they are formed. Because rocks form around plant and animal remains, finding the age of the rock is another method of discovering the age of the fossils in it.

◀ WHAT MAKES SOME MATERIALS RADIOACTIVE?

Some materials give out invisible rays called radioactivity. Some of the rays are like X-rays.
Others are streams of tiny particles. They come from atoms in the material that break apart.

At the center of every atom is a nucleus. It is made up of very small particles called protons and neutrons packed tightly together. If the

material contains elements that have many protons and neutrons in the nucleus, it may be radioactive.

The particles do not like being packed together in large numbers, so some may leave the nucleus, making the element radioactive.

Two kinds of particles may be produced. Alpha particles are each made up of two protons and two neutrons. Beta particles are electrons produced by the break-up of neutrons.

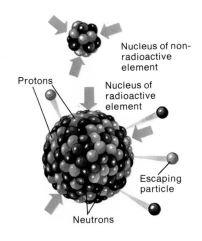

Nucleus of non-radioactive element
Protons
Nucleus of radioactive element
Escaping particle
Neutrons

65

▲ HOW DO LASERS WORK?

A laser produces a very thin but very powerful beam of colored light. Inside the laser is a material like a crystal. It is fed with light or other kinds of energy, which it releases as very bright light.

The material that produces the light from a laser is called an active material. The first lasers had a ruby crystal. Now special glass rods and tubes of dyes and gases are also used.

The active material receives energy from a pumping source. The energy that it pumps in may be electricity or light. This energy is absorbed by the atoms, which are raised to a high-energy state. Then all the atoms lose this extra energy at the same moment by producing light of exactly the same color.

The material has a mirror at one end so that the light emerges in a thin beam from the other end. Some lasers produce invisible infra-red rays instead of light.

▶ HOW FAST DOES LIGHT TRAVEL?

Light moves at a speed of over 186,000 miles per second. It takes light just over a second to reach us from the Moon and eight minutes to travel to the Earth from the Sun. It takes years for light to get to us from the stars.

The speed of light in space is 186,288 miles per second. It travels at a slightly slower speed through air, water and other transparent materials.

Other kinds of rays similar to light also travel at the same speed. They include radio and television signals, infra-red or heat rays, ultraviolet rays and X-rays.

The speed of light is thought to be the fastest possible speed at which anything can travel. Because a spaceship could not travel faster than light, no matter how powerful it was, it would take many years to travel to even the nearest star.

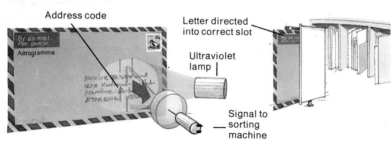

Address code

Letter directed into correct slot

Ultraviolet lamp

Signal to sorting machine

▲ HOW IS ULTRAVIOLET LIGHT USED?

Ultraviolet light is a form of light that is invisible. However, if it strikes certain materials called phosphors, it makes them glow. It is used to sort letters by machine, and to identify forged documents and paintings.

In England, letters arriving at a postal sorting office are given address codes in the form of patterns marked in pale or invisible inks containing phosphors. In the sorting machine, an ultra-violet lamp causes the pattern to light up. The code is "read" by the machine, which sends the letter to the correct compartment for delivery.

In ultraviolet light, inks and paints look very different from their appearance in ordinary light, and this can show up a forgery.

Some ultraviolet light reaches us from the Sun. This tans us and also produces vitamin D in the skin, which prevents a bone disease called rickets.

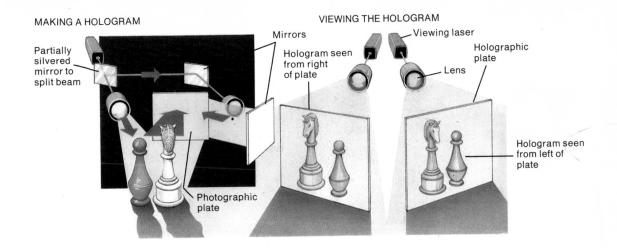

MAKING A HOLOGRAM

Partially silvered mirror to split beam

Mirrors

Photographic plate

VIEWING THE HOLOGRAM

Hologram seen from right of plate

Viewing laser

Holographic plate

Lens

Hologram seen from left of plate

▲ WHAT ARE HOLOGRAMS?

Holograms are amazing pictures that appear to have depth just like real objects. For example, if you look at a hologram of the front of a cube and then move to one side, you will see the sides of the cube just as if you were walking around it! Holograms are made with lasers.

To make a hologram, the object is lit by light from a laser. This light reflects from the object and strikes a photographic plate placed nearby. At the same time, the laser beam is split so that it also reflects from mirrors and strikes the plate directly.

The plate is then developed. A black-and-white pattern appears on it, producing a holographic plate. When one side of this plate is lit up by a laser beam and it is viewed from the other side, an image of the object appears behind the plate.

The image is in three dimensions, just like the real object, but in the color of the laser light. Projection holograms can be projected by lasers to appear in front of the holographic plate. There are also special holograms that can be seen by daylight.

▶ HOW ARE X-RAYS PRODUCED?

When you have an X-ray, a machine sends a quick burst of X-rays through a part of your body such as your mouth or chest. The X-rays are invisible and you feel nothing. The rays then strike a piece of photographic film. When it is developed, an image of the inside of your mouth or chest appears on the film.

The X-ray machine contains a filament that is heated to produce a stream of electrons. A high-voltage power supply fed to the X-ray machine accelerates the electrons in a beam towards a metal target.

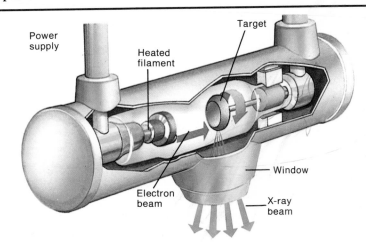

Power supply

Heated filament

Target

Electron beam

Window

X-ray beam

As the electrons are stopped by the target, they give out X-rays.

The X-ray beam leaves the machine through a window, and goes through the patient's body. The rays pass through flesh more easily than teeth or bones, which cast X-ray shadows. A film pack is placed next to the part of the body to be examined, and the X-rays penetrate the wrapping and expose the film.

Alternatively, the rays produce an image on a fluorescent screen, which is rather like a television screen.

▶ WHY DO THINGS LOOK NEARER UNDERWATER?

If you try to pick up an object in a tank or pool of water, you'll find that it is deeper than it looks. The reason for this is that light rays from the object bend as they leave the water.

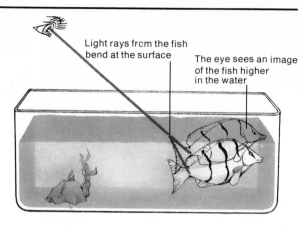

Light rays from the fish bend at the surface

The eye sees an image of the fish higher in the water

Rays of light from an object travel up through the water to the surface. As they move from the water into the air, the rays bend towards the surface of the water. The light rays then travel to the eyes.

However, our eyes always assume that light travels from anything we see in a straight line without bending. We see the object in the position it would have if light traveled in a straight line to the eyes. It therefore appears to be higher in the water.

◀ HOW DOES A MAGNIFYING GLASS WORK?

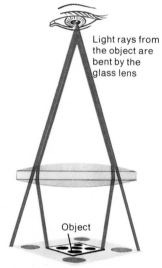

Light rays from the object are bent by the glass lens

Object

The eye sees an enlarged image

Light rays from an object pass through the magnifying glass to reach your eyes. The glass bends the rays, which reach your eyes as if they were coming from a bigger object.

The magnifying glass is a lens. Refraction causes light rays passing through a lens to bend at the surfaces between the air and the glass. The glass is a convex lens, which bends light rays from all points on the object towards each other. However, the eye believes that the rays have come from the object in a straight line without bending. This causes an enlarged image of the object to appear behind the glass.

A magnifying glass can also project an image on a piece of paper. You can make an image of the Sun appear and burn the paper. This is because the glass bends all the Sun's rays passing through it so that they meet on the paper and form an image.

▶ HOW DOES A MIRROR WORK?

When you look in a mirror, light rays go from you and strike the mirror. The rays bounce off the mirror and come back to your eyes. You see an exact image of yourself, but it is reversed.

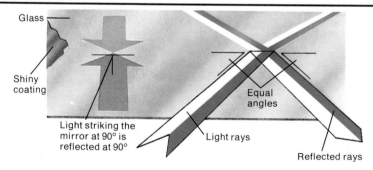

Glass

Shiny coating

Light striking the mirror at 90° is reflected at 90°

Light rays

Equal angles

Reflected rays

A mirror is made of glass with a shiny coating on the back. The light rays pass through the glass and are reflected from the coating.

Light rays are reflected back by a flat mirror at the same angle as they strike the mirror. This makes an image seen in a flat mirror appear to be the same size and shape as the object.

However, the image is always reversed. This is because light rays from the right side are reflected back on this side. In the image, you see the object's right side to your right. But if you were to see the real object in the same position as the image, its right side would be to your left.

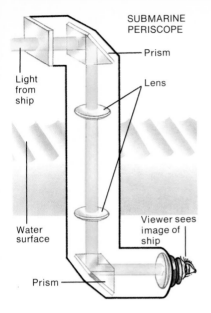

SUBMARINE PERISCOPE

Prism

Lens

Light from ship

Water surface

Viewer sees image of ship

Prism

▲ HOW DOES A PERISCOPE WORK?

You can use a periscope to see something from a higher level as if you were taller. A simple periscope has two sloping mirrors, one above the other. Light from an object strikes the top mirror, which reflects it to the bottom mirror. This mirror reflects the light into your eyes, and you see an image of the object.

A submarine has a periscope so that it can observe ships on the surface when it is submerged. This periscope works in the same way as a simple periscope, but has prisms instead of mirrors to give a high-quality image. It also has lenses to produce a magnified view of a ship on the surface.

Periscopes have many other uses. They enable people to look into parts of a machine or building that are sealed off or are dangerous to enter. In an emergency, an engineer can inspect a nuclear reactor or the hold of an aircraft with a periscope, for example.

▼ HOW MUCH CAN A MICROSCOPE MAGNIFY?

You can see objects highly magnified in an optical microscope. The most powerful microscope can make an object look as much as 2500 times bigger than it really is. Electron microscopes can make things look even bigger still.

At the bottom of the microscope, a mirror and condenser shine a beam of light through the object. The object is usually held between two thin plates of glass.

The focusing knob is then turned to bring the objective lens very close to the object. This lens makes light rays from the object meet. They form a magnified image of the object inside the tube of the microscope. The light rays go on to the eyepiece lens, which magnifies the image more.

The magnifying power is given by multiplying together the powers of the objective and eyepiece lenses. A microscope may have several lenses to give different magnifications.

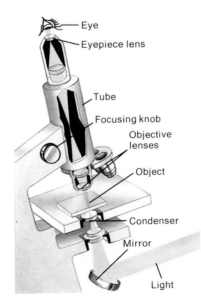

Eye

Eyepiece lens

Tube

Focusing knob

Objective lenses

Object

Condenser

Mirror

Light

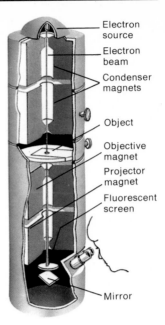

Electron source

Electron beam

Condenser magnets

Object

Objective magnet

Projector magnet

Fluorescent screen

Mirror

▲ HOW DOES AN ELECTRON MICROSCOPE WORK?

The electron microscope can magnify objects by as much as a million times. Instead of using light rays, it works with beams of tiny particles called electrons. The image is seen on a screen or may be photographed.

Optical microscopes cannot magnify more than about 2500 times because the light rays cannot produce a sharp image. Electron microscopes use beams of electrons instead of light rays. Electrons have a much shorter wavelength than light, which enables much greater magnifications to be achieved.

The electron microscope works like an optical microscope with a condenser and objective and eyepiece (projector) lenses. The lenses are powerful magnets or electrodes. They produce an electron image using a beam of electrons passed through the object. The projector forms this image on a fluorescent screen.

▲ HOW DO SOME OBJECTS FLOAT ON WATER?

If you are very careful, you can lower a needle on to some water and it will float on the surface. The surface of the water has an invisible "skin" over it. The needle is held by this skin so that it appears to float on the water.

In the water, the water molecules pull at each other with a strong force. This binds the molecules together so that the water remains a liquid.

The molecules at the surface pull more strongly because there are no water molecules pulling from above them. This forms a kind of surface barrier because the surface molecules also pull on the molecules of any object at the surface.

If the object is light, like a needle, then the pull of the surface water molecules stops it from sinking. This pull is called surface tension. It enables some insects, such as the pond skaters shown here, to walk across the surface of water.

▼ HOW DO PULLEYS WORK?

You can lift very heavy loads with a pulley. You pull on the rope, and the pulley wheels go around. The pulley is fixed to the ceiling or a support and lifts the load.

The weight of the load that can be raised with a pulley depends on the number of wheels and the way in which they are connected together. If the pulley has one rope, with a six-wheel pulley you can lift a load six times greater than you could without it.

The reason for this is that the amount of rope that you pull is six times as long as the distance that the load is raised. This increases the amount of force you apply to the load by six times and you can lift the load.

However, it does not increase the amount of effort or work involved. Work depends on the distance you move a load as well as its weight. Moving 200 pounds by one yard requires the same work as lifting 100 pounds by two yards.

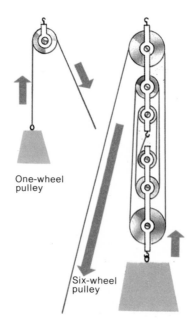

One-wheel pulley

Six-wheel pulley

Only about a tenth of the ice shows above the water

▲ HOW CAN ICE FLOAT IN WATER?

Ice floats on water because a piece of ice is lighter than the same amount of water. The ice is not very much lighter than the water, so it floats low in the water.

When water freezes to ice, the water molecules line up in rows. But as they do so, the molecules move apart slightly. The ice increases in size as it forms and this gives ice a lower density than water, making it float in water.

The force between the molecules is very strong, and nothing can resist the expansion that occurs as the ice forms. This is why water pipes sometimes burst in winter. The ice expands and cracks the pipe. Then when the weather gets warmer, the ice melts and water pours from the cracked pipe. It is unusual for a liquid to expand on freezing, but it is a good thing that water does so. The layer of ice that may form over lakes and the sea in winter prevents the water beneath from freezing.

▶ WHAT DO HYDRAULIC MACHINES DO?

HYDRAULIC JACK

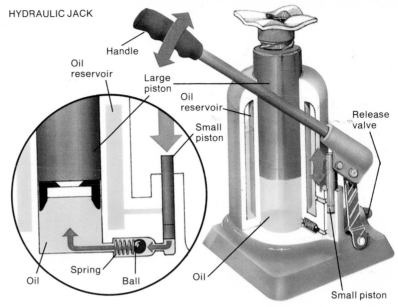

Hydraulic machines operate brakes on vehicles, presses and hammers for shaping metal objects, and lifting and digging machines. The hydraulic systems in these machines work with fluid at high pressure.

Hydraulic systems are used in machines that have to create a very powerful force over a short distance. For example, a hydraulic jack raises a large vehicle just off the ground.

A hydraulic system contains two pistons that move up and down in cylinders. The cylinders beneath the pistons are filled with a hydraulic fluid such as oil, and the cylinders are connected by a pipe. When

one piston is pushed down, it increases the pressure of the fluid throughout the system. The increased fluid pressure then raises the piston in the other cylinder.

The first piston is smaller than the second. But as the

fluid pressure is the same in both cylinders, the second piston rises with more force because it is bigger. However, to produce this pressure, the first piston has to move down a greater distance than the second piston is raised.

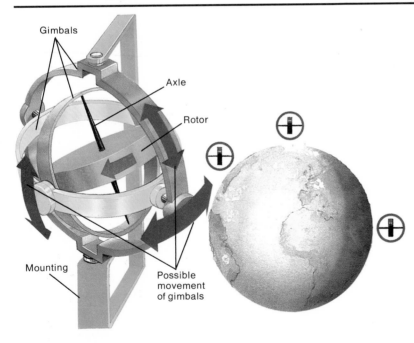

▲ HOW DOES A GYROCOMPASS WORK?

A gyrocompass shows the direction of north like a magnetic compass. But instead of using magne-

tism, it contains a spinning disk like a gyroscope. The axle of the disk always points north. A card marked with directions shows which way north lies.

The disk or rotor of the gyro-compass is powered by an electric motor so that it spins non-stop. The axle of the rotor always points in the same direction and it can be set to point north.

The rotor is mounted in gimbals that do not force it to turn. As the ship or aircraft changes direction, the gimbals turn so that the axle of the rotor still points north. This movement is transmitted to the compass card, which also turns to show the direction of true north.

Another kind of gyro-compass automatically sets itself north-south. It works like a gyroscope, which turns at right angles to the direction in which the axle moves. In the gyrocompass, the rotor turns in response to any movement of the axle away from true north and brings it back to true north.

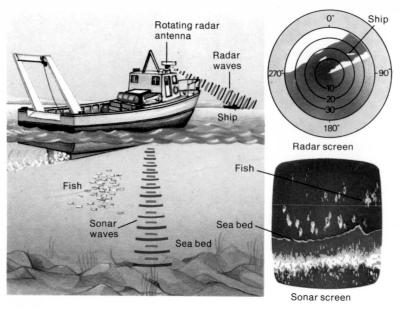

Radar screen

Sonar screen

▲ HOW DOES RADAR WORK?

Radar is a way of finding out how far away things are. A radar antenna sends out signals like radio signals. These bounce off a distant object and come back to the antenna. The radar set works out how far away the object is by measuring the time it takes for the signal to return.

Radar helps to guide ships and aircraft, especially at night and in fog. The radar sets can detect other ships and aircraft as well as the shore or the land below.

The antenna of the radar rotates, sending out signals in all directions. Returning signals go to a screen which displays the position of any object reflecting the signals. In this way, a radar map of the area surrounding the antenna is produced on the screen.

Airports use radar to check the positions of aircraft that are leaving or arriving at the airport. Controllers can see the aircraft on radar screens.

◀ HOW DOES SONAR WORK?

Sonar is used on boats and ships to find the depth of anything beneath them. Sonar can measure the depth of the sea bed as well as locate shoals of fish and submarines. It works like radar, except that sonar uses sound signals instead of radio signals.

A transducer under the boat or ship converts electric signals into pulses of sound that it sends down through the water. Any object in the water sends back an echo. The transducer receives the echoes, and turns them back into electric signals.

A receiver measures the time delay of the signals and their strength. This indicates how deep and how solid the objects are. It then displays the signals on a screen. It shows the depth on a scale and the solidity as a range of color. From this display, fishermen can spot shoals of fish and know how deep the shoal is and what kind of fish are in it. Sonar is also used to detect enemy submarines.

▶ HOW DOES A THERMOMETER WORK?

Inside a thermometer is a very narrow glass tube. At the bottom is a bulb containing a liquid. When the thermometer gets warm, the liquid expands and forces some of the liquid up the tube to a certain level. If it gets colder, the liquid contracts and falls.

The liquid in the bulb of a thermometer expands and contracts as the vibration of its atoms or molecules increases and decreases.

The silver liquid seen in many thermometers is mercury. If the thermometer contains a red or blue liquid, it is colored alcohol. Mercury expands more quickly than alcohol, so it shows the temperature faster. However, alcohol expands more than mercury so it can be used in a wider tube.

There are several other kinds of thermometers. Several of them convert heat into an electric signal that moves a pointer or lights up a digital display.

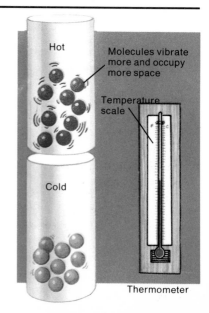

Thermometer

▶ HOW IS ULTRASOUND USED?

Ultrasound is sound that is so high in pitch that no one can hear it. It is used to scan babies before they are born, and in detectors that help blind people to find their way. It is also used in cameras that take sharp pictures automatically.

Ultrasound machines work in the same way as sonar. The machine sends out pulses of ultrasound that are reflected from an object. It receives the echoes and uses them to find out the distance of the object.

To inspect an unborn baby, ultrasound is bounced off the baby inside its mother. The echoes go to a machine that uses them to build up a picture of the baby on a screen, as shown here.

Blind people can use ultrasound detectors that give warnings of obstacles ahead. Some cameras send out beams of ultrasound to measure the distance of the things they are photographing. They then focus automatically.

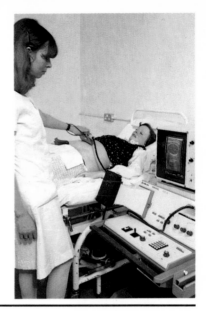

◀ HOW DOES A THERMOSTAT WORK?

A thermostat turns a heater on and off to keep the temperature constant.

Many machines that heat things need a thermostat. Irons, electric kettles, water heaters and cookers all use thermostats, because they work at a certain temperature.

Like the thermostat control of a heating system, these thermostats usually contain a strip made up of two layers of metal fixed together. When the strip gets hotter, the first metal expands more than the second metal. This uneven expansion causes the strip to bend. The controls on the thermostat are set so that the strip bends and operates a switch to cut off the heating system at the required temperature. Then as the room cools, the strip unbends and causes the switch to move back and cut in the heating system.

A heating element connected to the switch increases the bending of the strip.

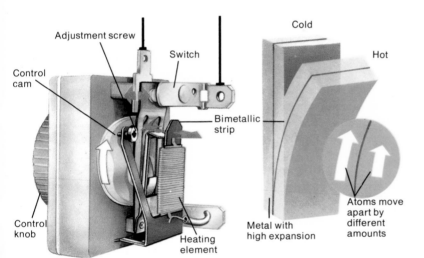

Adjustment screw · Switch · Control cam · Control knob · Heating element · Bimetallic strip · Cold · Hot · Metal with high expansion · Atoms move apart by different amounts

▲ HOW DOES METAL EXPAND AND CONTRACT?

When a piece of metal gets hot, it expands (gets bigger) in all directions. When it cools, it gets smaller (contracts). This happens because the tiny atoms inside the metal move apart as the metal gets hot. They move back together as it cools.

When a metal is heated, its atoms vibrate faster. The increased vibration acts against the forces that hold the atoms together and they move apart slightly.

As the metal cools, the vibration slows and the atoms pull themselves together again. The amount of expansion and contraction is small but its force is strong.

Electricity cables hang in a curve for this reason. If they were strung tightly between the pylons, contraction in winter would make the cables snap. Solids other than metals expand and contract too. Bridges have to be made with small gaps to allow for expansion in hot weather.

▶ HOW DO EXPLOSIVES WORK?

When an explosive goes off, the chemicals in the explosive suddenly produce lots of gas and heat. The hot gases expand in size very quickly. This gives the explosion its force and makes a wave of high pressure move out through the air.

High explosives like gelignite produce large amounts of hot gas very quickly to give a powerful instant explosion. The chemical reaction that occurs moves through the explosive at speeds of up to five miles a second.

High explosives are set off with detonators. These are small explosive charges that fit into the main explosive. A wire connects the detonator to a battery or other source of power. To set off the explosion, a current is sent to the detonator. It heats a wire inside the detonator and the detonator explodes, setting off the main charge. Low explosives like gunpowder do not need detonators.

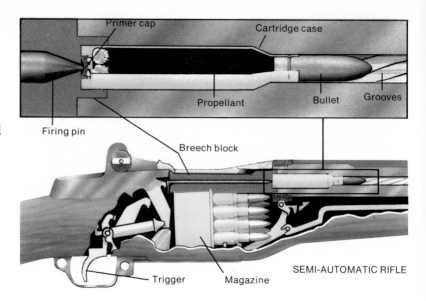

SEMI-AUTOMATIC RIFLE

▲ HOW DOES A RIFLE WORK?

Pulling the trigger of a rifle releases a spring. This makes a firing pin strike the base of a cartridge. The cartridge contains explosive and a bullet. The firing pin sets off the explosive, and the gas produced by the explosion makes the bullet fly out of the rifle.

In the cap of the cartridge is a primer that detonates to set off the charge of propellant in the cartridge case. Spiral grooves around the inside of the barrel cause the bullet to spin as it leaves the rifle. The spin stabilizes the flight of the bullet so that it points forward and does not tumble.

Automatic rifles contain a chamber of cartridges called a magazine. The force of the explosion throws the cartridge case from the breech block. It then raises another cartridge from the magazine into the firing position and fires it.

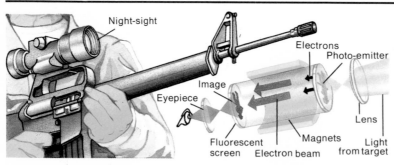

▲ HOW DOES THE NIGHT-SIGHT ON A GUN WORK?

Marksmen can see a target even at night. This is because there is always a little light even if it looks totally dark. The night-sight picks up this light from the target and makes an image of it appear on a small screen.

At the front of the night-sight is a lens. It focuses the very weak light rays coming from the target onto a metal disk called a photo-emitter. This disk produces electrons where it is struck by light rays. The electrons travel down the tube of the night-sight, and are focused into a beam by magnets around the tube. The beam strikes a fluorescent screen at the end of the tube, causing it to light up with an image of the target.

The marksman views it through the eyepiece of the night-sight to aim his rifle at the target. This kind of night-sight can brighten a target by fifty times, so that it becomes visible in total darkness.

▶ HOW DOES AN ATOMIC BOMB WORK?

An atomic bomb makes a huge explosion powerful enough to destroy a city. It contains pieces of uranium or plutonium instead of ordinary explosive. When the bomb is dropped, the pieces are fired together inside the bomb and it explodes.

When the pieces of uranium or plutonium meet, the nuclei of the atoms begin to break apart. A nuclear chain reaction occurs like that in a nuclear reactor (see page 64). However, the reaction is not controlled and a huge amount of energy is released.

To start the chain reaction, a critical mass of uranium or plutonium is formed. Stray neutrons in the mass start the chain reaction, and the mass contains enough atoms to keep the reaction going.

Instead of firing separate pieces of uranium or plutonium together to form the critical mass, a hollow sphere may be crushed into a solid lump by explosives.

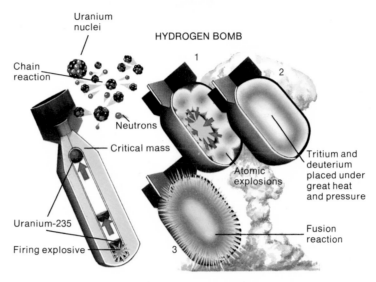

ATOMIC BOMB

HYDROGEN BOMB

Uranium nuclei

Chain reaction

Neutrons

Critical mass

Uranium-235

Firing explosive

Atomic explosions

Tritium and deuterium placed under great heat and pressure

Fusion reaction

▲ HOW DOES A HYDROGEN BOMB WORK?

A hydrogen bomb is so powerful that it needs atomic bombs to set it off. These atomic explosions cause an even more powerful nuclear explosion in a layer of hydrogen around the atomic bombs.

Around the atomic triggers of a hydrogen bomb are materials that produce forms of hydrogen called deuterium and tritium. The atomic explosions cause this fuel to be placed under enormous heat and pressure. A nuclear reaction called fusion then occurs.

The nuclei of the deuterium and tritium are forced together and they form nuclei of helium. This causes a loss of mass because the helium nuclei have less mass than the nuclei from which they form. The lost mass is converted into an enormous amount of energy and the bomb explodes.

▶ HOW DOES A MISSILE GET TO ITS TARGET?

A missile is a rocket with an explosive warhead. When the missile reaches its target the warhead explodes. The missile may chase the target if it is moving. The guidance system in the missile detects heat coming from its engine or uses radar. Other missiles are guided from the ground.

A radar system may track both the missile and its target. A computer reads the radar

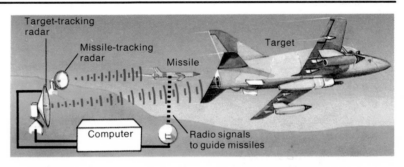

Target-tracking radar

Missile-tracking radar

Missile

Target

Computer

Radio signals to guide missiles

signals and controls the missile's guidance system to guide it to the target by radio.

Missiles may also be guided by operators linked to the missile by a long wire or by radio. Some missiles are able to follow a laser beam directed at the target by the operator.

Large missiles that are intended to destroy cities or missile sites fly on a set course.

Some missiles have computers containing maps of the land below. They can "see" where they are going and keep to the right course.

▲ HOW DO MOUNTAIN RAILROADS WORK?

The tracks of mountain railroads have three rails instead of the usual two. The third rail gives the locomotive extra grip on the track.

In mountainous areas, lines are often so steep that a locomotive's wheels cannot grip the track. To prevent the locomotive slipping backwards, a third, toothed, rail is laid in the center of the track, between the other two rails. This is called a rack rail.

Underneath the locomotive and each carriage is an extra wheel, called a pinion wheel. The cogs on the pinion wheels mesh with the teeth on the rack rail, and keep the train locked to the track.

On one Swiss mountain railway, up Mount Pilatus, the gradients are so steep (they average 1 in 2.75) that teeth are cut on each side of the rack rail rather than on top, and the locomotive and carriages have two pinion wheels.

▼ HOW DOES A STEAM LOCOMOTIVE WORK?

The locomotive produces steam in its boiler. This steam is used to power the engine, which drives the wheels.

Steam is produced by burning coal in the locomotive's furnace. Hot gases from the burning coal pass along tubes in the boiler and heat the water in it, producing steam. The steam passes through the regulator valve, which is controlled from the driver's cab. It is then superheated to put it under even greater pressure.

The pressurized steam enters the engine's cylinders through piston valves. Inside the cylinder, the steam expands and pushes the piston to the other end of the cylinder. The movement of the pistons is transferred to the locomotive's driving wheels by a series of rods.

Exhaust steam escapes up the chimney and into the air. Some of the steam is taken from the boiler to operate the brakes throughout the train.

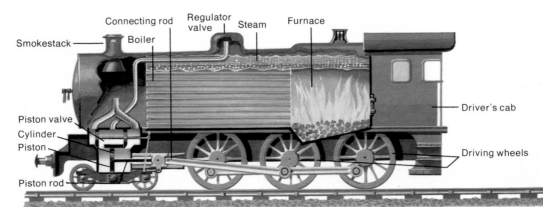

Connecting rod — Regulator valve — Steam — Furnace — Smokestack — Boiler — Driver's cab — Piston valve — Cylinder — Piston — Piston rod — Driving wheels

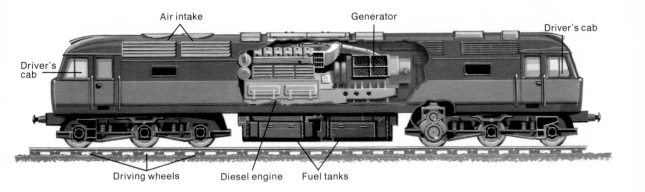

Air intake

Generator

Driver's cab

Driver's cab

Driving wheels   Diesel engine   Fuel tanks

▲ HOW DOES A DIESEL-ELECTRIC LOCOMOTIVE WORK?

The diesel engine drives a generator. The electricity the generator produces turns the locomotive's driving wheels.

Diesel engines produce power by burning a mixture of compressed air and diesel oil in their cylinders. This power has to be transferred to the locomotive's driving wheels. This is not done by means of gears, as happens in a road vehicle. Instead, electric transmission is used. The diesel engine drives a generator which supplies power to electric traction motors. These drive the loco-motive's driving wheels. The traction motors are mounted on the swiveling trucks.

Diesel-electrics are the commonest type of loco-motive. In most areas of the world, except southern Africa and parts of Asia, steam is scarcely used. Electric loco-motives are only profitable on very heavily used lines.

▼ HOW DO HIGH-SPEED RAILROADS OPERATE?

The maximum speed of passenger trains is usually about 100 miles per hour. But in some countries much faster services are available. These require specially developed locomotives and modified tracks. In some cases they run on separate lines not used by ordinary trains.

The best-known high-speed services are in France and Japan. In France, the *TGV* (*train grande vitesse*) started running between Paris and Lyons in 1981. In Japan, *Shinkansen* ("bullet") trains have been operating since 1964 and now link most of the major cities.

Both the *TGV* and the *Shinkansen* run on specially built lines. They are able to run at high speeds because no other trains use the lines.

There are no signals. Instead, the information the driver needs is displayed inside the cab.

Britain's Advanced Passenger Train has met several technical problems. Its tilting mechanism enables it to take curves safely at far higher speeds than normal. It will run on track used by other services, and therefore careful timing of the trains will be necessary.

Lift of wings

Drag of air

Thrust of engines

Weight of aircraft

▲ HOW DO AIRCRAFT FLY?

To fly, aircraft need power, which they get from their engines. They also need lift to raise them from the ground and keep them in the air. Lift is provided by the wings.

Aircraft wings are airfoils. They have a rounded upper surface and a flat underside. Their front edge is rounded and the back edge is tapered. As the plane moves through the air, the front edges of the wings split the air in two. One half moves over the rounded top edge, the other under the flat bottom edge. The air on top moves faster than the air underneath because it has further to travel. This reduces the pressure above the wing and creates lift.

At take-off, the aircraft's engines provide the power to generate lift. When the plane is flying at a constant speed, the lift from the wings equals the weight of the plane. The forward thrust of the engines balances the resistance, or drag, set up by the air.

▼ HOW IS AIR-TRAFFIC CONTROL ORGANIZED?

Air-traffic controllers make sure that planes take off and land safely and with as little delay as possible. They tell pilots exactly where to fly so that collisions with other planes are avoided.

When a plane is about 90,000 feet away from an airport and 2000 feet above it, it enters the terminal control area. Working from the traffic control center, which looks out on the runways, an air-traffic controller guides the pilot down, telling him at which speed and height to fly.

Radar provides air-traffic controllers with continuously updated information about the exact position, destination and identity of every plane, and about weather conditions.

The controller makes the final decision about which plane should land where.

Planes waiting to land are often "stacked" – they circle the airport in a vertical line. As a plane approaches the airfield, radio beams guide it to the runway. Air-traffic controllers are also responsible for aircraft taking off, and they often control planes throughout their flight from one city to the next.

Backward flight:
rotor blades tilted backwards

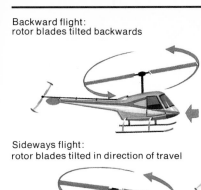

Sideways flight:
rotor blades tilted in direction of travel

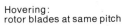

Hovering:
rotor blades at same pitch

Upward flight:
rotor blades at same pitch

Forward flight:
rotor blades tilted forwards

▲ HOW DO HELICOPTERS FLY?

Helicopters can fly in any direction, and even hover. The rotor blades control the direction.

The helicopter's engine drives the rotor. The blades of the rotor are airfoils, and they generate lift when they rotate. When a helicopter hovers, the blades all rotate at the same pitch. The weight of the craft balances the upward pull of the rotor.

To climb, the angle of attack of the blades must be increased. The angle of attack is the angle at which the leading edges of the blades meet the air. To move forwards, the blades are tilted forward. This increases their angle of attack at the rear of the helicopter but decreases it at the front, so pushing the craft forwards. Similar adjustments can make the helicopter fly in any direction.

The spinning of the rotor makes the helicopter itself rotate in the opposite direction. In most helicopters a tail rotor cancels this out.

▼ HOW DO PLANES TAKE OFF AND LAND VERTICALLY?

Vertical take-off planes go straight up into the air. They use the thrust developed by their jets to lift themselves or to land.

In normal jet planes, the jet engine is positioned horizontally. Air is sucked in at one end and mixed with fuel in a compression chamber. The exhaust gases stream out at the other end, thrusting the plane forward. Vertical take-off and landing (VTOL) planes make use of the same process, but their jets are positioned vertically. The exhaust is directed downwards and the resulting thrust is vertical.

VTOL craft are useful for military purposes, but less so for carrying passengers on commercial flights. Extremely powerful engines are needed for vertical take-off, and these leave less room for passengers and freight. VTOL craft are also very noisy. Some types of VTOL planes have separate engines to provide lift, or swiveling jets that can be positioned vertically or horizontally.

Forward flight:
jet nozzles point backward

Climbing:
jet nozzles point diagonally

Take-off, landing and hovering:
jet nozzles point downward

▲ HOW ARE SHIPS BUILT?

Ships are built in two main stages. First the shell is built. Then comes the fitting-out, when the machinery and equipment are installed.

Months of planning are necessary before the construction work can begin. First, a general design is agreed on. Then detailed working drawings of every single part are made. Often a computer does a lot of the detailed work. Sometimes a scale model is built and tested in a tank.

Now the ship starts to take shape. Sections of the hull are built in the shipyard and are brought to the building berth for assembly. Some ships are assembled from amidships in each direction. On others, workers begin at the stern and work towards the bows. Some parts, such as the propeller and the anchor, are made in another place.

The launch, when the ship slides into the water, is an occasion of great ceremony. The fitting-out takes place afterwards. This involves installing the engine, the plumbing, electrical and navigational equipment, lifeboats and so on. The ship is also furnished and decorated.

▼ HOW DO TRAWLERS FISH?

Trawlers fish with a large bag-like net called a trawl. They use it to catch fish such as cod, flounder, sole, hake and halibut.

The trawl may be over 300 feet long. It is let out on long warps, or ropes, from the stern to enormous depths, sometimes 5000 feet or more. The fish are swept in at the wide, open end and then get trapped at the narrower, closed end. Floats and large wooden weights called otter boards keep the mouth of the net open. When the net is full, powered winches haul it on board through a ramp at the stern.

Many modern trawlers are large factory vessels on which the fish are automatically gutted, filleted and frozen. There may even be a quality control laboratory.

▶ HOW DOES A SHIP'S PROPELLER WORK?

The propeller drives the ship through the water. Power is created by the ship's engines. It is transmitted to the propeller. The turning propeller converts the power into thrust for pushing the ship through the water.

Marine propellers usually have between four and seven blades, made of manganese bronze. As they turn, they speed up the movement of the water passing through them. The speeded-up water drives the ship forwards.

There are fixed and variable-pitch propellers. On fixed propellers, the angle of the blades cannot be changed. This means that the ship operates best only at her normal cruising speed. On variable-pitch propellers, the blade angle can be altered to suit the speed required and different weather conditions.

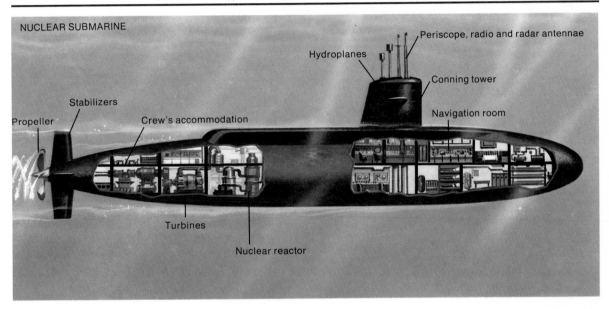

NUCLEAR SUBMARINE

Periscope, radio and radar antennae

Hydroplanes

Conning tower

Navigation room

Stabilizers

Propeller

Crew's accommodation

Turbines

Nuclear reactor

▲ HOW DO SUBMARINES WORK?

Submarines use small fins called hydroplanes to dive and surface. Ordinary submarines are powered by electric motors and diesel engines. Nuclear submarines produce their power in a nuclear reactor.

When the submarine wants to dive, its ballast tanks are flooded with sea water, and the hydroplanes are set to direct the craft downwards.

Once it is submerged, the hydroplanes are readjusted to control the angle of the dive. When the submarine has reached the right depth, the hydroplanes are set to horizontal, and small auxiliary ballast tanks are flooded.

The opposite happens when the vessel surfaces. The hydroplanes are set to direct the craft up. When it is close to the surface, compressed air is used to blow water out of the main ballast tanks. As the conning tower, which contains the periscope and is used for observation, breaks the surface, fresh air is sucked in to finish emptying the tanks.

Ordinary submarines use battery-powered electric motors while they are underwater and diesel engines when cruising on the surface. The diesel engines also recharge the batteries.

Nuclear subs use heat from a nuclear reactor on board to drive a steam turbine. The turbine also generates the electricity the vessel needs. Nuclear submarines can submerge for a long time.

A car engine creates the power that drives the car. The source of the car's power is its cylinders.

The pistons in the cylinders of the engine work on a four-stroke cycle. On the third stroke, known as the power stroke, a mixture of air and fuel vapor is ignited by an electric spark. The force of the explosion pushes the pistons down the cylinders. Most cars have four, six or eight cylinders, so this process is happening all the time, producing an even "flow" of power.

The rest of the engine captures the power and makes use of it to drive the car. The link is pistons-crankshaft-camshaft-distributor-transmission system. The pistons drive the crankshaft. A connecting rod between them converts the pistons' up-and-down movement into a circular movement. The crankshaft drives the camshaft, to which it is linked by a belt or chain. The camshaft drives the distributor, which distributes the electric current required to create the explosions in the cylinders. The crankshaft is also the link with the transmission system, which sends the power created by the engine to the car's driving wheels.

The various parts of the engine each have other important jobs. The camshaft controls the valves that let air and fuel vapor into the cylinders and get rid of the exhaust gases. The crankshaft drives the flywheel, to which the clutch is attached. To start the engine, you turn the ignition key.

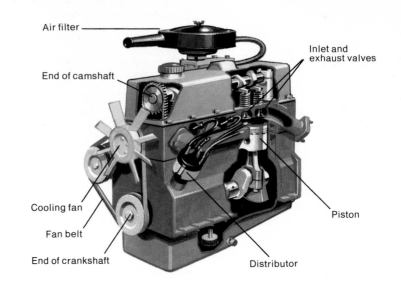

Air filter — Inlet and exhaust valves — End of camshaft — Cooling fan — Fan belt — End of crankshaft — Piston — Distributor

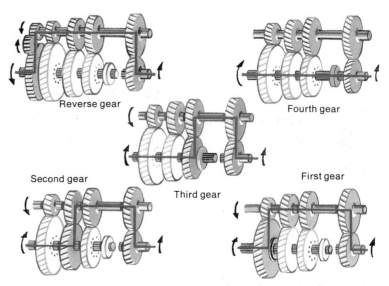

Reverse gear — Fourth gear — Second gear — Third gear — First gear

▲ HOW DO GEARS WORK?

Gears are part of the transmission system. This passes, or transmits, the power created by the engine to a car's wheels.

Car engines work best when the crankshaft is turning quite fast. This is when the car is traveling at speed and when fourth gear (also called direct drive), which sends power direct to the driving wheels, is used. When a car is moving slowly, gears are used to reduce the engine's speed without losing any of its force.

Power runs from the flywheel to the clutch, along three shafts in the gearbox and then to the final drive, which is connected to the driving wheels. A series of different-sized gear wheels is attached to each shaft, and power is transmitted through these.

When a driver changes gear, the correct gear wheels engage. Each gear reduces the engine's turning speed and increases its force.

▼ HOW DOES A CAR'S SUSPENSION SYSTEM WORK?

No matter how smooth they seem, road surfaces are in fact very bumpy. The suspension system absorbs the jolts.

Although tires absorb some of the bumps in the road, a car still needs a suspension system. There are several kinds, but they are mainly built of springs and shock absorbers. When the car hits a bump, the springs compress and absorb the shock. But a compressed spring must expand again and release the energy it has taken up.

The shock absorbers absorb the energy released from the spring and prevent the car from bouncing. In some cases, torsion bars are used instead of shock absorbers.

Most modern cars have independent front-wheel suspension. The suspension systems on the two front wheels work separately. If one wheel goes over a bump or a hole, the other is not affected.

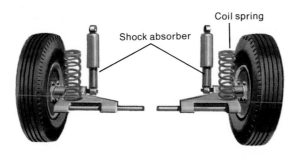

Coil spring
Shock absorber

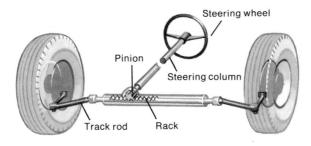

Steering wheel
Pinion
Steering column
Track rod   Rack

▲ HOW IS A CAR STEERED?

To steer a car, you turn the steering wheel in the required direction. The steering wheel is linked to the front wheels.

The steering wheel is at one end of the steering column. At the other is a toothed pinion wheel.

When you turn the steering wheel, the pinion wheel also moves and engages with a rack, which it moves from side to side. Short track rods send the movement of the rack to the front wheels.

Many large cars have hydraulic power-assisted steering. Cars are always steered by their front wheels. But their driving wheels, the ones to which power from the engine is transmitted, can be at the front or at the rear.

Power is sent to the driving wheels through the differential. This is a system of gears that allows the outer driving wheels to turn faster than the inner ones when cornering.

▼ HOW DO BRAKES WORK?

Good brakes are essential for safe driving. The driver operates them by pushing the brake pedal down.

Most modern cars have disc brakes, at least on their front wheels. When you press the brake pedal, the main brake cylinder begins working. This in turn controls "slave" brake cylinders on each wheel. The pistons in each slave cylinder press a pair of metal brake pads against a cast-iron disc, which stops the wheel going around.

The brake pads are the key to efficient braking, and they must always be kept in good condition. They have to grip the wheel in all temperatures, from below freezing point to very hot.

Many modern cars have power-assisted brakes, which increase the pressure a driver puts on the brake pedal.

Disc brakes are more efficient than old-fashioned drum brakes. In these, the slave cylinders press brake shoes against brake drums, which stop the wheels going round. The hand brake is used only for parking and is not used while the car is moving.

DISC BRAKES

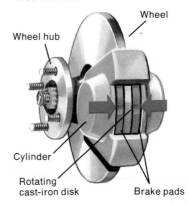

Wheel
Wheel hub
Cylinder
Rotating cast-iron disk
Brake pads

OUT IN SPACE

▶ HOW DO REFRACTING
TELESCOPES WORK?

A refracting telescope uses a lens known as the object-glass. This forms a small image of the object inside the tube. A much smaller lens, the eyepiece, is used like a magnifying glass to make the image look much larger.

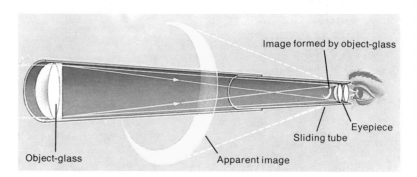

Image formed by object-glass

Object-glass

Apparent image

Sliding tube

Eyepiece

The object-glass shown in the illustration contains two lenses next to each other. This is because a single lens gives a colored image and blurs the details, whereas two lenses can be "achromatic", giving a sharp image with no false color. The eyepiece magnifies the image.

Binoculars work in the same way as an ordinary refracting telescope, but they contain glass prisms to "fold" the tube into a shorter length and to give an upright view.

▶ HOW DO REFLECTING
TELESCOPES WORK?

A reflecting telescope uses a special mirror, with a slightly hollow or concave surface, to form its image. A Newtonian telescope has a small flat mirror to reflect the light through the side of the tube, while a Cassegrain telescope sends it back through a hole in the main mirror.

Most amateurs use Newtonian telescopes, since they are cheaper than the Cassegrain kind. Also, reflecting telescopes are cheaper than refracting ones if the aperture is more than four inches or so (the aperture is the diameter of the main mirror or object-glass). The larger the aperture of a telescope, the fainter are the stars it can detect, and the smaller is the detail it can show on the Moon or a planet.

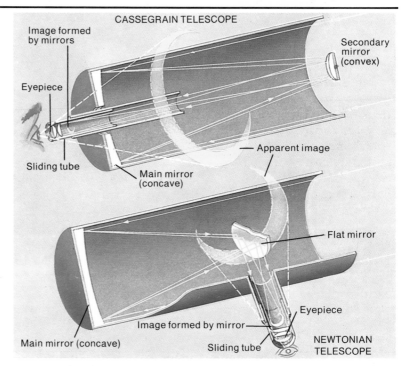

CASSEGRAIN TELESCOPE

Image formed by mirrors

Eyepiece

Sliding tube

Main mirror (concave)

Secondary mirror (convex)

Apparent image

Main mirror (concave)

Image formed by mirror

Sliding tube

Flat mirror

Eyepiece

NEWTONIAN TELESCOPE

The largest reflecting telescope in the world is in the Soviet Union. It has a mirror measuring 20 feet across, six times larger than the largest refracting telescope. Almost all big professional telescopes are Cassegrains, since the tube can be shorter than in the Newtonian telescopes. The Space Telescope (to be launched in 1985) will be a Cassegrain reflector.

► HOW DOES A TELESCOPE FOLLOW THE STARS?

The Sun, Moon, planets and stars all appear to revolve around the Earth once a day. But this is an illusion: it is the Earth's daily rotation that makes them appear to move. So an astronomical telescope must turn once a day in a direction opposite to the Earth's spin.

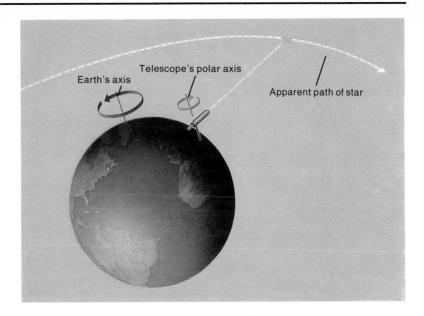

To do this, the telescope is built on an equatorial mounting or stand. The most important feature is the polar axis, which is set exactly parallel to the Earth's axis. The angle between the ground and the polar axis is equal to the observer's latitude, and, in the Earth's northern hemisphere, the polar axis points towards the Pole Star.

The other axis, the declination axis, is used only when pointing the telescope to start with. After this has been adjusted, rotation around the polar axis keeps the object in view. This can be done by hand, or with an electric motor.

► HOW DOES A RADIO TELESCOPE WORK?

Radio waves, like light waves, can be reflected. But the mirror is a metal sheet, or can even be wire mesh. A radio telescope usually has a very large hollow or concave dish, which reflects the signals from space onto the radio antenna.

A radio telescope produces recordings on magnetic tape, or a line on a graph, instead of a picture. Radio waves are given out by all sorts of objects in the universe, but the strongest emitters are certain very distant galaxies known as quasars. In our own galaxy, one of the most powerful radio sources is the Crab Nebula in the constellation Taurus. This is the remains of an exploding star or supernova, visible in daylight in the year 1054.

▲ HOW DO WE GET PICTURES OF OBJECTS IN SPACE?

Any telescope can be used as a camera. The object-glass (in a refracting telescope) or the mirror (in a reflecting telescope) forms an image of a planet or star in the sky. If this image is projected on to photographic film, the telescope can be said to be used like a camera.

Most modern professional telescopes are just huge cameras. The main difference with astronomical photography is that the film may have to be exposed for an hour or more. The longer the exposure, the fainter the stars that will be recorded. But even an ordinary camera, if it is guided to follow the turning sky, can record thousands of stars in a five-minute exposure.

APOLLO MOON-ROCKET (SATURN 5)

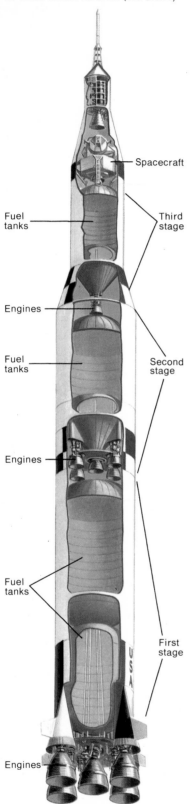

- Spacecraft
- Fuel tanks
- Third stage
- Engines
- Fuel tanks
- Second stage
- Engines
- Fuel tanks
- First stage
- Engines

USA

◄ HOW IS A SPACECRAFT LAUNCHED?

To escape from the Earth, a rocket must travel at seven miles per second. A single craft could not carry enough fuel to reach this speed: it would be too heavy to leave the ground! So a spacecraft has separate stages, which jump clear as the lower ones use up their fuel.

Normally, a three-stage rocket is powerful enough to launch an interplanetary probe. For example, the *Apollo* Moon-rocket at lift-off weighed about 3000 tons (as much as a hundred large trucks), but over 2000 tons of this was fuel for the huge first stage, which took it only about 56 miles off the ground. Once this had fallen back to Earth, the craft had enough fuel left to take it all the way to the Moon and back.

Smaller rocket engines may need more stages. The Indian satellite *Rohini*, launched in 1980, required a four-stage rocket powered by solid fuel.

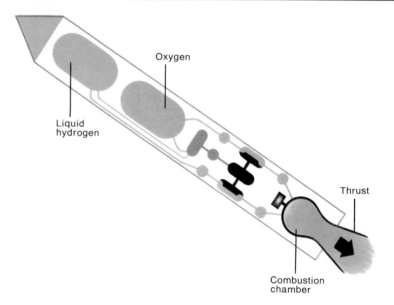

- Oxygen
- Liquid hydrogen
- Thrust
- Combustion chamber

▲ HOW DOES A ROCKET MOTOR WORK?

On the Earth, we usually move by pushing or pulling against something fixed. But in space there is nothing to push or pull against, so movement must be by reaction. A bullet fired from a gun kicks the firer backwards: hot gas leaving a rocket kicks the spacecraft forward.

Gunpowder rockets can work only in the atmosphere, since the gunpowder fuel needs air in order to burn. A space rocket has to use two fuels that react explosively when they are mixed together. One of these fuels is usually oxygen, stored as a bitterly cold liquid, turning into gas as it passes out through a valve. The other fuel is usually kerosene or liquid hydrogen.

The famous Saturn rocket, which sent men to the Moon and launched the USA's interplanetary probes, uses kerosene as the first-stage fuel, and hydrogen for the other stages.

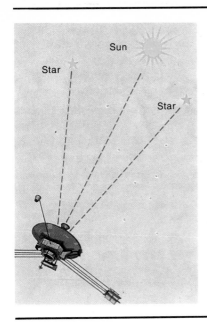

◀ HOW DOES A SPACEPROBE NAVIGATE?

As a space vehicle travels through space, the Sun appears to move across the stars, just as a traveler on the Earth sees nearby buildings appear to move across more distant ones. A computer calculates where the Sun and stars should be, if the spacecraft is on course.

These observations are made by special telescopes fixed to the craft, but a system of inertial guidance is also used. If a large wheel is set spinning rapidly, it is very hard to move its axis. Like a spinning top, it wants to remain in the same plane. Three wheels, spinning at right angles to each other, keep a platform inside the spacecraft fixed in the same plane, so that course alterations can be measured when the motors fire.

The wheels used in the *Voyager* spacecraft were made so accurately that they would keep spinning for 36 hours if their motors were switched off!

▶ HOW DOES A SATELLITE STAY IN ORBIT?

If we imagine a fantastically powerful gun on the top of a very high mountain, firing bullets at different speeds, three things could happen. The bullet could land on the ground far below (1); it could fly off into space (2); or it could curve exactly round the Earth and become a satellite (3).

To stay in orbit near the Earth, a satellite must travel at about five miles per second (28,000 kilometres per hour). Once it has gone into orbit, it will remain circling almost indefinitely. However, if it is less than about 125 miles above the Earth, the slight dragging effect of the Earth's outer atmosphere will cause it to lose speed and height, and after a few years it may burn up like a meteor.

A large satellite is braked more easily than a small one. The three-man *Skylab*, launched in 1973, fell to destruction from its orbit after only seven years.

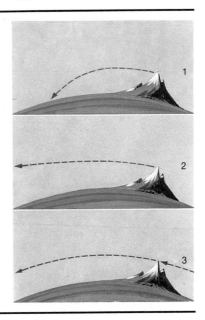

◀ HOW DOES A SPACECRAFT RETURN TO EARTH?

All spacecraft must find a way of slowing down from a speed of many miles per second to give the crew, or cargo, a soft touch-down. The landing is usually done by parachute, but the Space Shuttle glides down.

The return of the *Apollo* craft was an example of high-speed atmospheric braking. It hit the atmosphere at a speed of seven miles per second, the outer skin turning white-hot with friction. In a few minutes, the speed had dropped to 60 miles per hour, and it landed gently in the ocean by parachute.

The Shuttle, on the other hand, fires its engines in reverse to slow its orbital speed and it coasts down into the atmosphere at about four miles per second. It gets rid of this speed by banking and rolling along a path that takes it halfway around the world, landing at about 200 miles per hour.

Return of Apollo

Return of Space Shuttle

▼ HOW DO ASTRONAUTS BREATHE IN SPACE?

Our air contains several different gases. The most important one is oxygen, since this is what we must breathe in order to live. So astronauts have to take an oxygen supply into space, both in their cabin and in their spacesuits.

The Earth's atmosphere contains about 78% nitrogen, a harmless gas which dilutes the oxygen. A pure oxygen atmosphere in a spacecraft can be dangerous, because a single spark could cause an explosion. This happened when three American astronauts were testing an *Apollo* module, and they died in the resulting fire. Soviet spacecraft use a mixture of oxygen and nitrogen.

Another problem is how to get rid of the waste carbon dioxide that is breathed out. This could suffocate the astronauts if it builds up. It can be absorbed by chemicals, but on a very long flight it would be essential to extract and recycle the oxygen so that it could be used again.

◄ WHY ARE SPACESUITS PRESSURIZED?

When deep-sea fishes are brought to the surface, their eyes puff out because the pressure of the deep sea is no longer pushing on them. We do not realize it, but the atmosphere presses on us with great force. Even if we could breathe out in space, we would swell up and die an agonizing death.

The atmosphere at the Earth's surface produces a pressure equal to the weight of a large truck on each square yard. We do not notice this, since it is equal both inside and outside our bodies. But if the air inside a metal can is forced out by boiling water inside it, the can collapses under this pressure.

An unprotected astronaut would not only die by swelling up. His blood would also start to boil. The temperature at which a liquid boils depends on the atmospheric pressure. At a height of 6 miles (the height of Mount Everest) water boils at 165°F. Above about 12 miles, blood boils below body temperature. At zero pressure, the astronaut's blood would instantly turn to a deadly foam.

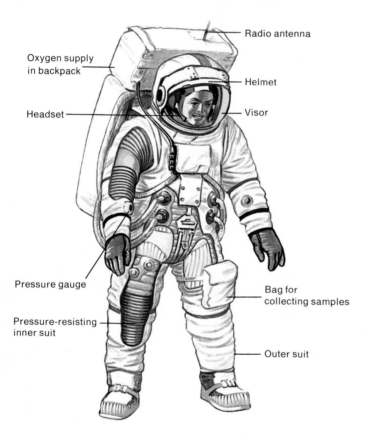

Radio antenna — Helmet — Visor — Oxygen supply in backpack — Headset — Pressure gauge — Pressure-resisting inner suit — Bag for collecting samples — Outer suit

▲ HOW DO ASTRONAUTS SPEAK TO EACH OTHER?

If they are outside the spacecraft or on the Moon's surface, they have to speak by radio, since sound cannot travel in empty space. However, if they are in the atmosphere of the cabin, they can talk normally to each other.

Communication between astronauts and the Earth can be a complicated matter, since our spinning planet regularly carries a single receiving station out of range of the spacecraft. So it is necessary to have several stations spread across the Earth's surface, so that one of them is always in contact with the spacecraft. Communication blackouts happen when a spacecraft is entering the Earth's atmosphere at high speed. The fierce heat strips the oxygen and nitrogen atoms, creating an electrical barrier.

◄ HOW DO ASTRONAUTS MAKE SPACE WALKS?

The term "space walk" is not very accurate. A person can walk only if he is on the surface of a planet, where gravity pulls his feet down onto the ground. In space, an astronaut can only float alongside his spacecraft.

The first space walk was made in March 1965 by one of the crew of a Soviet *Voskhod* satellite, A. Leonov. He remained outside for 24 minutes. Like all space-walkers, he was tied by a safety line. One of the most important walks was made in 1973, when the crew of the American satellite *Skylab* had to repair a damaged heat shield that made the craft dangerously hot.

▶ WHAT POWERS A SPACECRAFT'S EQUIPMENT?

All spacecraft use electricity. They may have batteries which are kept charged from the Sun's energy. These craft always have large solar panels which collect the Sun's heat. Electricity can also be "manufactured" specially.

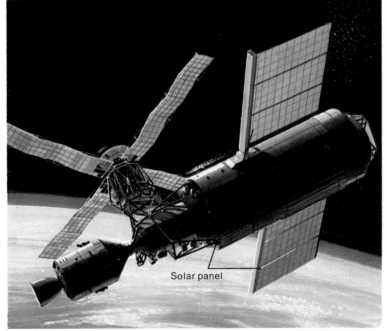

Solar panel

Spacecraft which are going to have to operate for many years usually depend on solar panels, since the Sun is such a reliable and constant source of energy. But it cannot help a space probe traveling towards the outer planets, where sunlight is weak. The *Voyager* craft use small nuclear-power packs, which will last them at least as far as the planets Uranus and Neptune.

Another source of electricity is the fuel cell, in which hydrogen and oxygen combine with each other to produce electricity and water.

The water by-product is useful for manned spacecraft, but the reaction can be dangerous. An exploded fuel cell wrecked the *Apollo 13* Moon mission.

▶ HOW DO WE MEASURE THE DISTANCE TO THE MOON?

The speed of light is very accurately known: it is 186,287 miles per second in space. If a light beam is aimed towards the Moon and reflected back, the distance to the Moon can be worked out.

This method requires a large telescope. Its mirror is used rather like a searchlight's reflector to transmit light pulses towards special reflecting panels left by astronauts on the Moon. Although the total journey only takes 2½ seconds, electronic timers can calculate the length of time to an accuracy of a few millionths of a second. By making many measurements, the Moon's distance is known to within a few feet.

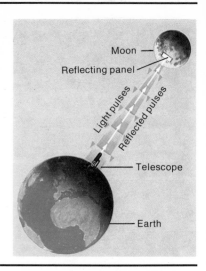

◀ HOW WAS THE MOON FIRST EXPLORED?

The first man-made object to hit the Moon was the Soviet probe *Luna 2*, in September 1959. The far side was photographed by *Luna 3* (shown here) in the same year. The first close-up photographs of the Moon's surface were taken by the American spaceprobe *Ranger 7* in 1964.

The first soft landings on the Moon were made in 1966, by spacecraft with automatic instruments. American space scientists considered their *Surveyor* landers only as a preparation for the later manned landings. But the Russians have continued sending unmanned probes: first the *Luna* landers, which have launched rock samples back to the Earth for detailed examination, and later the *Lunokhod* mobile devices.

▶ HOW DO UNMANNED SPACE VEHICLES WORK?

Several different kinds of unmanned spacecraft have been sent to the Moon. Some went into orbit around it and took detailed photographs. Others have landed on the surface and tested the conditions there, sending messages by radio to the Earth.

The Soviet "lunar rover" or *Lunokhod* is the most advanced unmanned vehicle. Weighing about a ton, it has television cameras to let the operators see where it is going. It can start and stop at will, turn corners, and take samples of the lunar dust.

Two *Lunokhods* have so far been sent to the Moon by *Luna* space vehicles, while three others (*Lunas 16, 20, and 24*) have returned to the Earth, carrying surface samples. *Luna 24* dug to a depth of 6½ feet. The upper part of the spacecraft is fired from the Moon's surface, finally landing on the Earth by parachute.

90

Lunar rover

Lunar module

▲ HOW DID APOLLO GET TO THE MOON?

Apollo, **which made the first manned landing in 1969, had to travel in stages. First, it was shot up into Earth orbit; then it flew to the Moon and went into lunar orbit. The lunar module then descended to the surface, leaving the command module awaiting its return.**

Of the 3000 tons of space-craft that left the launching pad, only the 15-ton lunar module reached the Moon, and over ten tons of that was fuel. Apart from the launch itself, and the final splashdown in the Pacific, the most vital moments were when the lunar module landed, and when it rejoined the command module in lunar orbit.

The illustration shows the lunar module in the back-ground. The lower stage remained on the Moon, while the upper part, carrying the two astronauts, blasted free.

▲ HOW DID THE APOLLO ASTRONAUTS EXPLORE THE MOON?

The astronauts' most im-portant task was to collect samples of the lunar rocks and soil. In the first three missions, they explored by foot. In the last three, they used a lunar rover.

They also set up various experiments to be operated from the Earth. These included seismometers, to measure the tremors of the surface; devices to detect atomic particles from the Sun; cosmic dust detectors; and the special reflectors for measuring the lunar distance. These and other devices were set out on the surface around the central power package, a nuclear plutonium reactor capable of producing electricity for many years.

In the illustration, the astronauts are seen pushing tubes into the ground to collect samples. The six missions collected about 880 pounds of rock.

▲ HOW DID THE LUNAR ROVER WORK?

The lunar rover was a four-wheeled buggy driven by electric batteries. Its top speed was about 7 miles per hour, and it had enough power to travel about 40 miles before its batteries ran down. The last three *Apollo* flights took a rover.

The rover could carry two astronauts and about 400 pounds of cargo, including rock samples. It had several cameras fitted to its frame. A color television camera sent live pictures back to the Earth via the umbrella-like antenna. The wheels had metal treads to give them a good grip on the dusty surface, and both front and rear wheels could be steered, so that it could be turned very sharply.

The astronauts had to unpack it from the lunar lander, where it was stored folded up during the journey from the Earth.

▶ HOW WAS MARS EXPLORED?

The first close-up photographs of Mars were taken by *Mariner 4* in 1965, but better ones were taken by *Mariner 9*, which went into orbit around Mars in 1971. In 1976, two *Viking* spacecraft landed on the surface and took detailed photographs and measurements.

Both *Viking* craft landed in Mars' northern hemisphere, *Viking 1* at latitude 23°, and *Viking 2* at latitude 48°. Even at *Viking 1*'s site, the temperature never rose above −27°C, and at night it fell to −65°C.

Each craft picked up soil samples and tested them for living organisms, but nothing similar to Earth-like germs or bacteria was found. The landscape was a desert covered with boulders and the sky, instead of being dark blue as expected, was turned pink by a dust haze. *Viking 2* continued to transmit information until March 1980, while *Viking 1* operated until November 1982.

▶ HOW ARE THE OUTER PLANETS EXPLORED?

Two series of spacecraft have visited the planet Jupiter and beyond. *Pioneer 10* passed close to Jupiter in 1973. The following year, *Pioneer 11* also examined Jupiter and went on to pass Saturn in 1979. In the same year, *Voyagers 1* and *2* passed Jupiter, and they have now visited Saturn. *Voyager 2* is expected to pass Uranus in 1986.

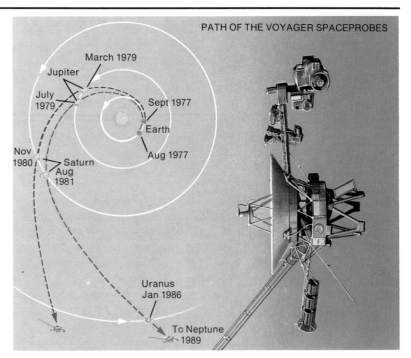

PATH OF THE VOYAGER SPACEPROBES

These deep-space craft have sent back photographs of the outer planets that are truly amazing, when we consider how far away they are and how long they have had to keep working. In addition to cameras, they also carry instruments to examine the chemical elements of the planets, their magnetic fields, and the particles sent out by the Sun. Both craft carry their own computer, although their instruments are operated by commands sent from tracking stations on the Earth.

It is fortunate for us that the outer planets are lined up nicely for a "tour". If Jupiter and Saturn happened to be on opposite sides of the Sun, separate probes would have had to be sent to the two planets. Also, *Voyager* probes used Jupiter's tremendous gravitational pull to "sling" them toward Saturn.

▼ HOW IS THE SPACE SHUTTLE LAUNCHED?

The Shuttle is launched into space attached to two booster rockets and a huge fuel tank. As it reaches a height of about 27 miles, the two booster rockets parachute back to Earth. To return, the

Shuttle fires its engines to head Earthwards, and glides down.

Everything about the Shuttle is re-usable, except for the giant fuel tank. This is jettisoned after the craft reaches orbit, falling back into the Indian Ocean. Once this has been detached, the

Shuttle's only rocket power comes from small engines that fire for about 2½ minutes to begin its descent. To get rid of its speed of about 6 miles per second, it is taken through a series of steep turns as it enters the upper atmosphere, where the outer skin is heated by friction to about 3630°F.

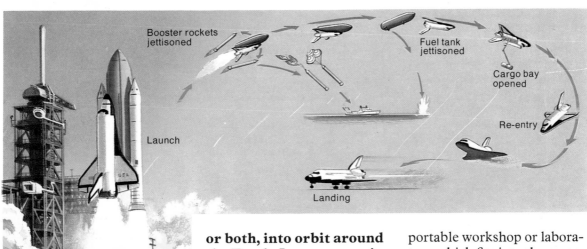

Launch
Booster rockets jettisoned
Fuel tank jettisoned
Cargo bay opened
Re-entry
Landing

▲ HOW IS THE SPACE SHUTTLE USED?

The Space Shuttle is a "workhorse". Its job is to carry astronauts, or cargo,

or both, into orbit around the Earth. It can carry six passengers, and has a cargo bay 60 feet long and 15 feet in diameter.

By 1985, the Shuttle should be operating at full capacity. One of its most important uses will be to carry Spacelab into orbit. Spacelab is a

portable workshop or laboratory which fits into the cargo bay. Different teams will equip their own Spacelab, and book a flight. The workshop remains in the Shuttle until it is time to descend once more.

Another very important task for the Shuttle will be to carry the big Space Telescope into orbit, a flight planned for 1985.

▶ HOW WILL THE SPACE TELESCOPE WORK?

The Space Telescope, which should be launched into orbit in 1985 by the Space Shuttle, will have a mirror measuring eight feet across. It will be about ten times as powerful as any telescope now in existence.

The Space Telescope will be completely automated. It will be pointed to different objects by radio messages from the

ground, and the photographs it takes will be transmitted down to the Earth by radio.

It will have an enormous advantage over ground-based instruments; the sky will always be clear, and its images will be much sharper. It may even help to detect large planets orbiting around nearby stars. It will certainly bring into view remote galaxies that are undetectable with our present instruments. Knowledge of the universe is certain to take a tremendous jump forward.

▼ HOW ARE OCEAN CURRENTS MEASURED?

The simplest way to measure the speed and direction of currents at the surface of oceans is to record the movement of floating objects such as icebergs. But the most accurate way to measure flow is to use a current flow meter.

There are many kinds of current meters. Most have a vane to keep the meter in line with the current flow, a compass to record direction and a propeller, which is turned by moving water and records the current speed.

Electronic equipment can make other measurements, such as temperature and salt level. These are recorded on tapes. Several flow meters are attached to one cable to measure currents at different depths.

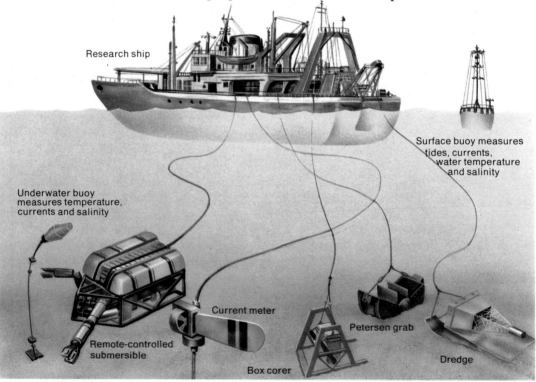

Research ship

Surface buoy measures tides, currents, water temperature and salinity

Underwater buoy measures temperature, currents and salinity

Current meter

Petersen grab

Remote-controlled submersible

Box corer

Dredge

▲ HOW ARE SAMPLES COLLECTED FROM DEEP OCEANS?

In the past, scientists had to rely on simple dredges to collect samples. The picture shows some modern equipment. Remote-control samplers can be sent down to the sea bed. Powered submersibles can reach the deepest parts of the ocean and scoop up samples.

The research ship *Glomar Challenger* is equipped to drill deep into the ocean floor four miles below the waves.

A sonar beacon is lowered to the sea floor. This sends messages to on-board computers which keep the ship in one place by auto-matically working the propeller and side thrusters. The drill bit, corer and pipes are lowered to drill into the sea floor. A re-entry funnel enables the drill to be lifted, replaced and returned to the same hole. As the drill bites into the sea bed, the layers of sediment and rock are collected in a core barrel and brought to the surface to be studied.

▶ HOW ARE HIGH-ALTITUDE WINDS MEASURED?

Radio-sonde balloons are sent high into the atmosphere several times a day from many weather stations. The balloon is filled with hydrogen, so it rises quickly. It carries with it a tiny radio transmitter which sends back information about the weather. The course of the balloon can be tracked by radar. High-flying aircraft and satellites also send back information.

Radio-sondes send back information about temperature, pressure and humidity as well as winds. The balloon bursts when the pressure gets too low, and the instruments are parachuted back to Earth.

From balloons, aircraft and satellite information, we know that there are strong winds at five to nine miles above the Earth's surface. They are called jet-streams, and can travel at 185 to 250 miles per hour. Aircraft can save time and fuel by flying along in jet-streams moving in the same direction.

◀ HOW ARE HURRICANES EXPLORED?

In 1943 an aircraft flew through a hurricane for the first time. Now, hurricanes can be photographed from satellites and tracked by radar. But detailed information still comes from specially equipped aircraft.

Intense storms in the Atlantic are called hurricanes. In the Pacific they are called typhoons, and in the Indian Ocean they are cyclones.

In the USA, aircraft explore hurricanes by flying right through the storm and its "eye". On board, scientists study radar and other instruments. They record wind speed (both vertical and horizontal), wind direction, temperature, pressure and cloud particles. Computers record the information, which is sent by satellite to the National Hurricane Center in Miami. Instruments may be parachuted into the sea to obtain more measurements. Aircraft are checked for damage after every flight.

▶ HOW IS SEA-FLOOR SPREADING MEASURED?

Scientists now know that in parts of some deep oceans, rock is being added to the sea bed from below the crust. This widens the sea floor and pushes the continents apart very, very slowly.

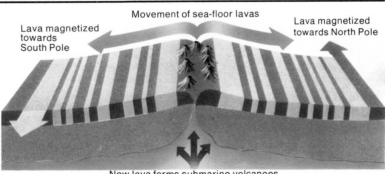

Movement of sea-floor lavas

Lava magnetized towards South Pole

Lava magnetized towards North Pole

New lava forms submarine volcanoes

This theory is checked by collecting samples of sediments and rocks from deep below the oceans. Their structure, fossils and magnetism are studied to discover their age. As samples are collected across the width of an ocean, the pattern of the age of the sea-floor can be mapped.

In the Atlantic Ocean the pattern is very clear. The newest rocks are in the Mid-Atlantic Ridge, a vast range of submarine volcanoes. Studies show that the Atlantic is getting wider and that Europe and America are slowly drifting apart.

▶ HOW DO SATELLITE PICTURES TELL US ABOUT EARTH?

A lot of satellites are circling our globe. Some send back photographs, such as those used in weather forecasting. Others send back images using visible light and infra-red light. Computers can turn these into pictures of the Earth.

The *Landsat* carries a special scanner which senses the light and heat reflected from the Earth below. Information is relayed back to special ground-receiving stations and converted into pictures like the one shown here.

From *Landsat* pictures we can study the land use of any part of the Earth. Floods can be predicted and pollution warnings given. Because heat differences are measured, warm and cold sea-currents can be mapped. Pictures from *Landsat's* infra-red readings can be processed to show the health of growing crops, the effects of drought or types of surface rock.

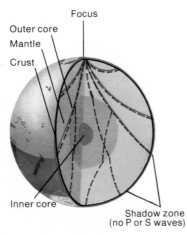

- – – – – Primary (P) waves
- ――――― Secondary (S) waves
- ▬▬▬▬ Long (L) waves

▲ HOW CAN SCIENTISTS "SEE" INSIDE THE EARTH?

Scientists tell us that the inside of the Earth is in layers: the crust, the mantle, the outer core and the inner core. Evidence for these has come from seismology, the study of earthquakes.

Seismographs record three different kinds of earthquake waves. Primary (P) waves travel fastest and can pass through solids, liquids or gases. Secondary (S) waves

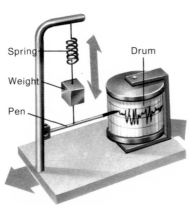

Red arrows show direction of movement caused by a seismic wave

travel through solids only. Long (L) waves are slowest of all as they only travel along the surface. Long waves do most damage.

Geologists are especially interested in P and S waves. Their speed and path change with the density of the rocks. P waves speed up in the mantle, slow down in the outer core, and speed up again in the inner core. S waves will not pass through the outer core. This suggests it is like a liquid. The waves change direction as they pass from one layer to another.

◀ HOW ARE EARTHQUAKES MEASURED?

Earthquakes cause *seismic* waves to travel through the Earth. These are recorded on a seismograph. Scales are used to measure their intensity. The Richter Scale measures the strength of an earthquake. The higher the number, the more severe the earthquake.

The seismograph is firmly embedded in a masonry column which reaches down to solid rock. The weight is attached to the support by a tie-wire or spring. Attached to this weight is either a pen or a beam of light which makes a mark on paper covering the rotating drum. When an earthquake occurs, the weight stays still, while the rest of the seismograph moves.

The trace that is made on the paper round the drum records several kinds of shock waves. The time difference between the waves is noted. It is possible to work out how far away and how severe the earthquake is.

96

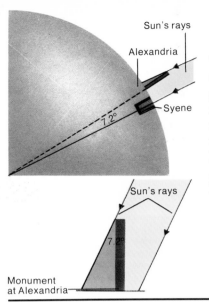

Sun's rays
Alexandria
Syene
7.2°

Sun's rays
7.2°
Monument at Alexandria

The science of measuring the Earth is called geodesy. When people realized that the Earth is round, they were able to measure it by using their knowledge of circles and angles (geometry). Nowadays, geodimeters can measure long distances very accurately, by using light rays.

The diagram shows how, in about 250 B.C., Eratosthenes measured the Earth's circumference. At noon in midsummer, the Sun shone straight down a well at Syene, near Aswan in Egypt. At the same time in Alexandria, a monument showed that the Sun made an angle of 7.2°. Using geometry, Eratosthenes knew that the angle at the center of the Earth would be the same. He calculated that the Earth's circumference was 28,770 miles.

Eratosthenes was not far out. In fact, the distance around the equator is 24,903 miles.

▶ HOW ARE DIFFERENT KINDS OF ROCK FORMED?

Geologists put the rocks of the Earth's surface into three main groups: igneous (meaning "fire-formed"), sedimentary (made from sediments) and metamorphic (meaning "transformed").

The first rocks of the Earth's crust were igneous, made from molten material which cooled down. These rocks were eroded, and the particles were deposited as sediments in the sea or on land. These became sedimentary rocks. Rocks that were subjected to great heat and pressure were transformed into metamorphic rocks.

Rocks are still being formed today. The Earth's surface is being worn away by rivers, which carry mud and sand to the sea where sediments build up. They are squeezed and cemented into rocks such as clay and sandstone. Rocks move downwards at the edges of crustal plates and are metamorphosed, or changed. Igneous rocks rise to the surface from volcanoes.

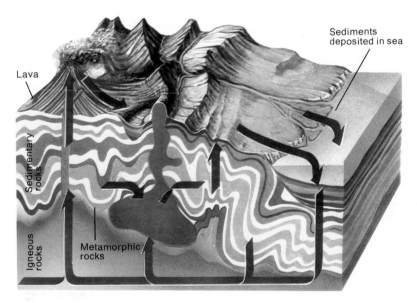

Lava

Sedimentary rocks

Igneous rocks

Metamorphic rocks

Sediments deposited in sea

▲ HOW CAN WE MEASURE THE AGE OF ROCKS?

From a study of the rock layers (strata) and of any fossils they contain, geologists can work out the order in which rocks were formed, but not their age. Normally, the lowest strata are the oldest. The age of some rocks can be worked out by measuring the decay of their radio-active elements.

Radioactive elements gradually change into different elements. For example, uranium gradually changes into lead. This rate of change can be measured. Rock samples can be analyzed to see how the radioactive elements have changed, and this gives some idea of their age.

Radioactive elements like uranium-238 and potassium-40 take hundreds of millions of years to decay. Tiny amounts are found in igneous rocks and can be used to date some Pre-Cambrian rocks. Fossils of the last few million years can be dated using carbon-14.

PLANTS AND ANIMALS

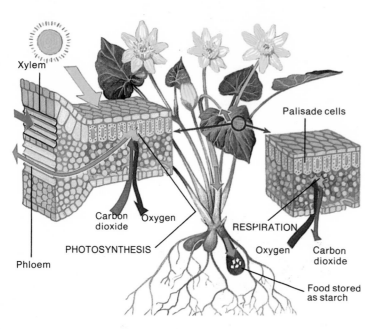

Xylem

Palisade cells

Carbon dioxide Oxygen

RESPIRATION

PHOTOSYNTHESIS

Oxygen Carbon dioxide

Phloem

Food stored as starch

▲ HOW DO PLANTS MAKE FOOD?

Plants make food by photosynthesis. Using light energy, carbon dioxide and water, they build up food sugars.

Photosynthesis relies on the green pigment chlorophyll, which captures the Sun's light energy. It is contained in tiny structures called chloroplasts. These are most numerous in the upper (palisade) layer of cells in each leaf.

Chlorophyll converts light energy into chemical energy, which fuels the chemical reactions of photosynthesis. Carbon dioxide, taken from the air, and water are used to build up sugar, which is carried to other parts of the plant by the phloem tissue of the vascular bundles. It is stored in the form of starch.

▲ HOW DO PLANTS BREATHE?

Plants take in oxygen. They use it to break down food sugars, releasing energy and carbon dioxide. This process is called respiration.

The process of respiration is basically the opposite of photosynthesis. The sugars that the plant built up during photosynthesis are broken down again, using oxygen, into carbon dioxide and water. The energy released in the process is used for other activities of the plant, such as growth and reproduction.

Respiration takes place in tiny cell structures called mitochondria. About 40 per cent of the energy stored in the food sugar is converted into chemical energy. The rest is lost as heat.

▼ HOW DOES A SEED GROW INTO A PLANT?

A seed begins to germinate when water soaks through the hard seed coat. The seed swells and starts to grow a root and a stem.

As germination begins, the young root, or radicle, grows from the seed first. As it grows the young stem, or plumule, develops.

The young seedling is nourished by food reserves, or endosperm, which in many seeds is contained in the seed leaves, or cotyledons. Sometimes, as in sunflower seeds, the growing stem carries the cotyledons above the ground. There they turn green and carry on photosynthesis until the first true leaves develop. In other seeds, such as broad beans (shown here), the cotyledons remain underground.

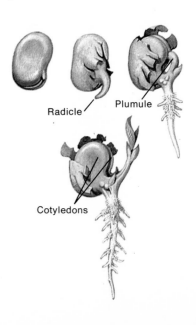

Radicle Plumule

Cotyledons

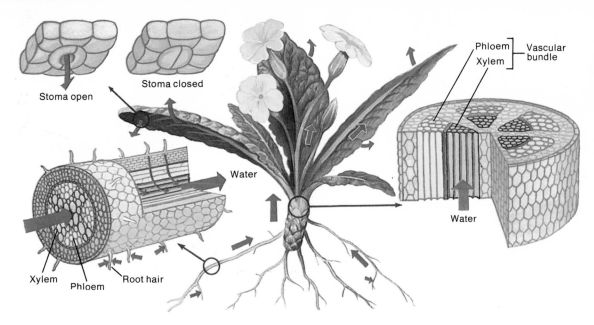

Stoma open

Stoma closed

Water

Xylem

Phloem

Root hair

Phloem
Xylem

Vascular bundle

Water

▲ HOW DO PLANTS GET WATER?

Plants take water from the soil. Fine roots and root hairs collect the water, which passes on to other root cells.

The roots of a plant have two functions. First, they anchor the plant firmly in the ground. Second, they seek out and take up the water that is so essential for the plant.

Plants have several different kinds of root systems. Some spread out horizontally near the surface. Others go down deep into the soil.

The plant takes in water near the tips of the finest roots and through root hairs. These are single, long cells that grow out from the root surface. From these cells it is drawn into the inner cells of the root. Finally, it enters the conducting tissue at the center of the root.

The conducting tissue is called the xylem. It forms a star-shaped column up the middle of the root. Water passes up the xylem to the stem.

▲ HOW DOES WATER TRAVEL UP THE STEM?

Water travels to the leaves up the xylem, or conducting tissue, of the stem. In a green-stemmed plant, the xylem vessels are contained in a number of bundles, known as vascular bundles.

Water-conducting xylem vessels are non-living, tube-like cells. They are open at both ends and many cells are joined together to form long conducting tubes that run the whole way up the plant.

It was once thought that water was pumped up the stem, either by the roots or by living cells in the stem. However, this has been shown to be impossible. Scientists now believe that the water is drawn up the stem from above. Water molecules exert an enormous pulling force on each other. Evaporation of water from the leaves, or transpiration, creates a partial vacuum. Water from the leaf veins moves in to fill this vacuum. As it does so, it draws more water up.

▲ WHAT IS TRANSPIRATION?

Transpiration is loss of water from the leaves. Water evaporates from the leaf cells and diffuses out through tiny pores called stomata.

Losing water by evaporation from its leaves helps to keep a plant cool. On a hot day a large tree can reduce its temperature by several degrees. But in the process it loses several hundred gallons of water. More importantly, transpiration causes the plant to take up water from the soil, bringing minerals with it.

The rate at which a plant transpires varies according to the outside conditions. On hot, dry days plants transpire very quickly. Dry winds also increase the transpiration rate. On cool days, and when the air is moist, plants transpire more slowly.

The rate of transpiration can also be controlled by the stomata. When there is little water available in the soil and the plant is nearly wilting, the stomata close.

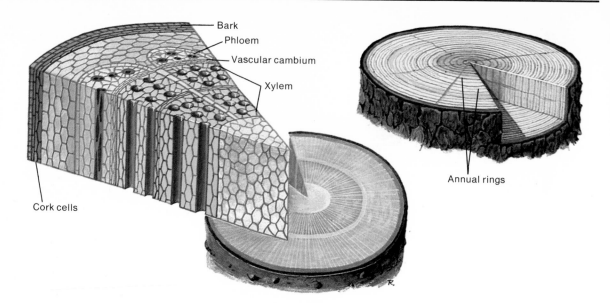

Bark
Phloem
Vascular cambium
Xylem
Cork cells
Annual rings

▲ HOW IS WOOD FORMED?

The wood of a tree is its water-conducting tissue, or xylem. Each year more wood is added and the trunk becomes thicker.

The vascular bundles of a young shoot are arranged in a ring. Each bundle contains phloem and xylem and, between them, a layer of cells called the vascular cambium. The cells of the cambium are able to divide and produce new xylem and phloem.

A stem starts to become woody as cambium develops in between the bundles. At the same time it produces new xylem tissue, which forms a cylinder inside the stem.

Each year the cambium produces more xylem and the woody shoot increases in thickness. The xylem cells are tough and have greatly thickened walls, which gives the shoot strength.

In older branches and the main trunk of a tree the wood in the center becomes blocked up. Water conduction is left to the outer wood, or sap-wood, while the central core provides immense strength.

▲ HOW CAN YOU TELL THE AGE OF A TREE?

If you look at a tree stump you will see a series of rings. Each one represents one year's growth. So by counting the rings you can find the age of the tree.

A tree grows only during the spring and summer. In spring the cambium produces large xylem cells. But gradually, as summer passes, the new xylem cells become smaller. In late summer or early autumn growth stops until the next spring, when large cells are produced again. The difference between small, late summer cells and large spring cells shows up clearly as a growth ring. And the number of growth rings therefore shows how many seasons have passed since the tree first began to grow.

The cambium also produces new phloem cells each year. But, unlike xylem cells, they do not form growth rings. Phloem cells are soft and thin-walled. As each year's new phloem develops, the old phloem is crushed and becomes part of the bark.

▲ HOW IS BARK FORMED?

As a young shoot becomes woody on the inside, bark forms on the outside. Bark is composed of non-living, waterproof cells.

As wood is laid down inside a shoot, a layer of cells near the outside begins to divide and produce "cork" cells. The walls of these cells soon become heavily thickened with a waterproof substance. The cells die and form bark.

Over the years the bark is constantly added to from the inside. So as the diameter of the twig, branch or trunk increases, the waterproof barrier is maintained. But the outer bark often splits and cracks or becomes flaky.

Bark gives a tree protection against the weather and sudden temperature changes. It contains substances that repel insects and it resists fire. Bark often has commercial uses. True cork comes from the bark of the Mediterranean cork oak. The drug quinine comes from the bark of cinchona trees and cinnamon comes from the bark of the cinnamon tree.

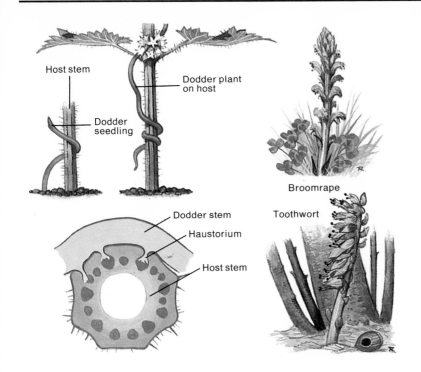

Host stem

Dodder plant on host

Dodder seedling

Broomrape

Toothwort

Dodder stem

Haustorium

Host stem

▲ HOW DO PARASITIC PLANTS GET THEIR FOOD?

Parasitic plants depend entirely on their hosts for their nourishment. They have no green leaves and so cannot photosynthesize food. Instead they bore into the tissues of other plants and take the food they need.

Parasitic plants are those that live on other plants without giving any benefit to their hosts in any way. In some cases, parasites cause harm to their hosts.

Dodders are one of the largest groups of parasitic plants. They have long, twining red or yellow stems, with tiny scale-like leaves. Most dodders live off small plants, such as nettles or gorse, but some are parasites of trees. A young dodder seedling quickly twines round a host plant, and buries its suckers (haustoria) into it in as many places as it can.

Broomrapes and toothworts are also common parasites. Broomrapes attack such plants as clover and daisies, while toothworts are parasites of trees, such as hazel. Both of these parasites attack the roots of their hosts.

One of the most extra-ordinary parasites is *Rafflesia*. Its huge flower, the largest in the world, is the only visible part of the plant. The remainder consists of threads buried in the host's roots.

▶ WHY DOES MISTLETOE GROW ON TREES?

Mistletoe grows high up in the branches of trees to be as near to the light as possible. To help it survive, it takes the water it needs from the sapwood of its host tree.

Host wood

Haustorium

The mistletoe plant is a partial parasite. It can be found on several kinds of tree, such as apple, hawthorn, willow, poplar and lime. It is not a total parasite because it has green leaves and makes its own food by photosynthesis. But it does take water and nutrients from its host.

Mistletoe seeds are spread by birds, which feed on the white berries. The sticky seeds may be wiped off the birds' beaks on to host branches, or may fall on to the branches in the birds' droppings.

After a seed has germi-nated, the young seedling develops a tough, wedge-shaped structure called a haustorium, which pushes into the host's sapwood. Meanwhile the mistletoe plant develops a disk-like structure that clamps onto the outside of the branch.

Mesquite · Century plant · Prickly pear · Saguaro · Ocotillo · Evening primrose · Barrel cactus · Creosote bush · Night-blooming cereus

◀ HOW DO SOME DESERT PLANTS SURVIVE DROUGHT?

A number of desert plants avoid drought altogether. Their seeds only germinate after rain.

During dry periods the seeds of many desert plants lie dormant in the ground. But after a rainstorm they quickly germinate, flower and die.

In North America, dry valleys may suddenly be covered with the blooms of the California poppy and evening primrose.

▲ WHY ARE MANY DESERT PLANTS FLESHY?

Another way of surviving drought is to store water. Many desert plants store water in their stems and leaves.

A great deal of water can be stored in fleshy leaves and stems. After a rainstorm, a barrel cactus may double its diameter. To cut down loss of water due to transpiration, cacti have no leaves. Instead, they have spines, which also serve to keep away animals.

Desert plants that store water in their leaves are also common. The century plant has a rosette of tough, sharply pointed leaves. Pebble plants have a pair of fleshy leaves that look like pebbles.

Many desert shrubs, such as ocotillo, shed their leaves in times of drought, growing new ones when the rains return. Prickly pear cacti and chollas sometimes shed the ends of their stems.

The root systems of desert plants are also important. Cacti have shallow roots, but they spread out over a wide

area. The root tips of a saguaro may be as far as 50 feet from the stem. Mesquite, on the other hand, has very deep roots that can reach over 100 feet down to find water.

The creosote bush is an unusual desert plant. Its leaves shrivel up in dry conditions, but they revive again after rain. Creosote bushes defend their water-collecting territory. Their roots give out poisons that prevent other plants, even their own seedlings, from growing too close.

▶ HOW DO ALPINE PLANTS SURVIVE THE COLD?

Alpine plants are mostly small and they often have coverings of hair.

Alpine plants have to survive biting cold winds, low rainfall and poor soil. Generally, alpines are small and low-growing. For example, the leaves of the alpine aster are all close to the ground. Many alpines are ground-hugging cushion plants.

Generating warmth is important. The temperature

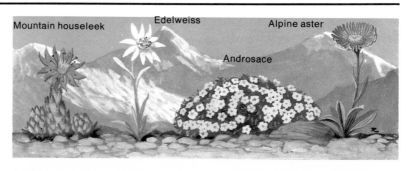

Mountain houseleek · Edelweiss · Alpine aster · Androsace

inside a cushion plant is often much higher than the outside temperature. Some alpines, such as gentians, generate their own warmth, which allows them to grow beneath the snow in spring.

Some alpines are covered in

hair; edelweiss is a well-known example. This not only keeps the plant warm but also helps to protect the plant from strong sunlight and to conserve water. Several alpines, such as houseleeks, store water in fleshy leaves.

▶ HOW DO SALT-MARSH PLANTS SURVIVE?

Salt water kills most flowering plants. But salt-marsh plants have special adaptations that enable them to tolerate these conditions.

A salt-marsh occurs where a river deposits mud along the banks of an estuary. A number of plants live in this salty mud. Others live higher up, in the drier, less salty regions of the salt-marsh.

Salt water usually draws water out of plants, which die as a result. But salt-marsh plants have unusually high amounts of salt in their cells. So they can actually take in water from sea water. Many salt-marsh plants store water in fleshy leaves or stems.

The most salt-tolerant plant is glasswort, which can stand being completely covered at high tide. Higher up the salt-marsh are plants such as seablite, sea aster and common salt-marsh grass. On the drier ground are such plants as salt-marsh rush, sea lavender and sea milkwort.

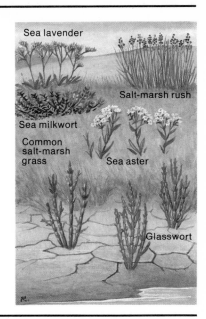

Sea lavender

Salt-marsh rush

Sea milkwort

Common salt-marsh grass

Sea aster

Glasswort

◀ HOW DO SOME PLANTS STING AND SCRATCH?

Some plants defend themselves against plant-eating animals. Plant defenses include thorns, spines, prickles and stings.

Picking thistles or holly can be a painful business. The edges of their leaves are armed with sharp spines. Gorse and cacti go even further; their leaves are modified into spines. Plants such as blackthorn, hawthorn and acacia, defend themselves with thorns. These are formed from modified twigs. The prickles of roses and brambles also grow on the stems. They are produced by the outer layer, or epidermis.

Some plants, such as comfrey, bugloss and prickly pear cacti, produce tiny bristles that cause intense irritation. Others have stinging hairs. A nettle sting consists of a hollow hair with a hard bead on the end. When it is touched, the bead breaks off. The hair pierces the skin and poison is pumped in.

Hawthorn

Gorse

Bramble

Nettle

▶ HOW DO CLIMBING PLANTS HOLD ON?

Climbing plants climb by using tendrils, hooks or suckers. Or they may just coil around other plants.

Most plants put a lot of energy into growing strong stems in order to reach the light. Climbing plants save this energy and use the stems of other plants for support.

The prickles of roses and brambles enable them to cling on and ramble up and over other plants. Ivy grows up trees and buildings by putting out tough, penetrating aerial roots. Some climbers, such as bindweeds and honeysuckle, coil around their hosts.

Other plants have special grasping organs. Some vetches, for example, have tendrils at the ends of their leaves. Other plants, such as gourds and many vines, have long tendrils that grow out of their stems.

Old man's beard and other species of clematis grasp hold of supports by coiling their leaf-stalks. Virginia creepers have tendrils with sticky pads.

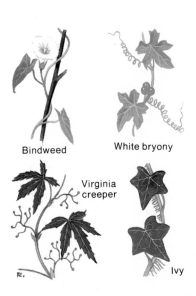

Bindweed

White bryony

Virginia creeper

Ivy

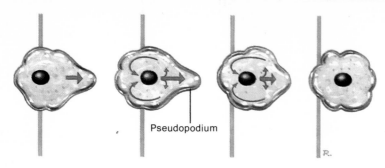

Pseudopodium

▲ HOW DOES AN AMOEBA MOVE?

An amoeba moves by first putting out a *pseudopodium*, or "false foot". Then the rest of the animal's body follows on behind it.

The main part of an amoeba's body is made of a grainy liquid called endoplasm. Outside this, just inside the outer membrane, there is a thin layer of clear, jelly-like material called ectoplasm.

When an amoeba starts to move, the ectoplasm becomes liquid at a certain point and the animal starts to put out a pseudopodium. A stream of endoplasm moves up the center of the animal into the pseudopodium. There it spreads out and becomes firmer, adding to the ectoplasm at the sides. At the rear end the opposite happens so that the whole animal moves towards the pseudopodium.

We still do not know what causes the endoplasm to stream forward. But scientists think that the "rear" end of the animal contracts and squeezes the animal forward.

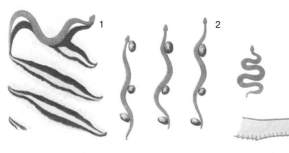

▲ HOW DO BIRDS FLY?

When a bird flaps its wings through the air, it produces lift, like the wings of an aircraft. At the same time it produces forward thrust, which in an aircraft is produced by the propellers or jet engines.

In cross-section, a bird's wing is shaped in a similar way to the wing of an aircraft. It is slightly curved so that air passes more rapidly over the upper surface than over the lower one. This produces lift.

In flight the downstroke of the wing is the power stroke. The wing beats downwards and forwards and the inner part of the wing produces lift. The outer part of the wing, which has large flight feathers, produces even more lift and forward thrust. As the wing comes down, the flight feathers twist and curl upwards to act like propellers.

▶ HOW DO SNAKES MOVE?

Some snakes move in a series of leaps, using a movement like a concertina. Others pass waves down their bodies and others use the scales on their bellies. Sidewinding snakes move in a series of steps.

On rough ground most snakes move by passing waves of muscle movement down their bodies. The waves push against stones and other objects (2).

On smoother ground, a snake may move in a concertina fashion. The snake draws its body up into a series of bends. Then, keeping the tail region firmly on the ground, it throws its head and body forwards (3).

Some snakes can move in a straight line. Waves of muscle movement pass down the snake's belly (4).

Sidewinding snakes are usually found in the desert. They move over the sand in a series of sideways steps (1).

▶ HOW DOES A PARAMECIUM MOVE?

A paramecium swims through the water using its tiny hairs, or *cilia*, as "oars". It swims in a cork-screw fashion and finds its way by trial and error.

Cilia

The body of a paramecium is covered in diagonal rows of tiny hairs. The animal swims by beating these hairs, or cilia, backwards and forwards. When it is swimming for-wards, each cilium beats just after the one in front. This gives the impression of waves traveling down the animal.

Because the rows of cilia run diagonally across the body, the paramecium rotates as it swims. At the same time it travels in a spiral path through the water. It can swim over 500 times its own length (a hundredth of an inch) in one minute.

When a paramecium meets an object blocking its way, it reverses, changes its angle of approach slightly and tries again.

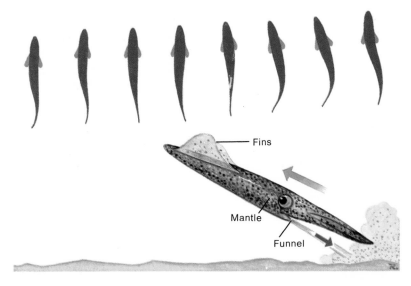

Fins

Mantle

Funnel

▲ HOW DOES A SQUID SWIM?

A squid swims by using jet propulsion. It squirts water out of its funnel and can move extremely fast.

On the underside of a squid there is a large chamber called the mantle cavity. It is surrounded by a muscular wall known as the mantle. The mantle cavity opens towards the animal's head and situated in the opening there is a short funnel.

The squid draws water into the mantle cavity through the opening. The mantle then closes against the funnel and contracts, or shrinks, forcing the water out through the funnel. The squid then moves in the opposite direction.

The funnel can be pointed either forwards or backwards, depending on which way the squid wants to go. The animal steers by means of its two fins.

Squid have highly stream-lined bodies and can push water out through their funnels with great force. As a result, they are very fast swimmers.

◀ HOW DO FISHES SWIM?

A fish swims by causing its muscles to contract, or shorten, all the way down its body. These push against the water and the fish moves forward.

When a fish swims, each part of its body moves from side to side. The contracting movement of the muscles travels in waves, which pass from the front to the rear of the fish. Many fishes also have a large tail to give them more forward thrust.

Most fishes control steering and braking with the front, or pectoral fins. However, this is not always so. Unlike bony fishes, sharks and their relatives do not have swim-bladders (air-filled sacs) to keep them afloat. So they have to propel themselves not only forward but also upwards. A shark uses its front fins, together with its specially shaped tail, to produce lift.

The strange puffer fish rows itself through the water using only its pectoral and dorsal fins. The tail fin is used as a rudder.

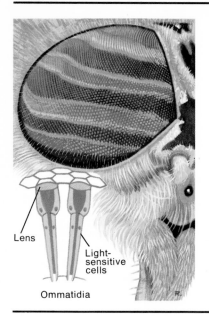

Lens

Light-sensitive cells

Ommatidia

◀ HOW DOES AN INSECT SEE?

The eye of an insect is made up of hundreds of tiny, separate units. Each one has its own lens and light-sensitive cells. Information from each unit passes to the brain, where an image is created.

The eye of an insect has many lenses, each of which directs light to its own group of light-sensitive cells. An insect's eye is therefore known as a compound eye.

The lenses lie on the surface of the eye and each one faces in a slightly different direction. Under a microscope, an insect's eye has many facets, or sides.

When the insect sees an object, it does so with several units, or *ommatidia*. But only one is actually facing the object and this is the only one that sees the image of the whole object. The surrounding ommatidia see only part of the object. This gives the insect information about the direction and shape of the object.

▶ HOW DO CATS SEE IN THE DARK?

Cats and other animals that hunt or feed at night have specially adapted eyes. As a result they can see in very dim light.

The eyes of mammals contain two kinds of light-sensitive cells. There are cones, which provide good vision in daylight, and rods, which are sensitive to dim light. A cat has a large number of rods in its eyes.

At night a cat's eyes have enormous round pupils to let in as much light as possible. In bright light the pupils narrow to thin, vertical slits to protect the sensitive rods.

Another feature of a cat's eyes is that they are very large, so that they can let in as much light as possible. At the same time they are shaped rather like a squashed tennis ball.

Finally, a cat has a layer of reflective cells at the back of each eye. This reflects back the light that has already passed through the retina once.

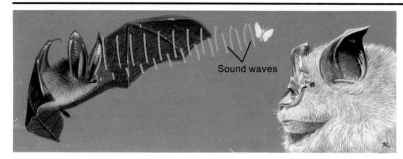

Sound waves

▲ HOW DO BATS FIND THEIR WAY IN THE DARK?

A bat does not have good eyesight, but is able to "see" by sound waves. It produces a series of high-pitched squeaks which are reflected back by the objects around it.

The way in which bats find their way about is called echolocation. They produce high-pitched squeaks that humans cannot hear. Some bats, such as the long-eared bat on the left, produce these sounds from their mouths. Others, such as the greater horseshoe bat, on the right, produce the sounds from their noses. The returning echoes are picked up by the bat's large, sensitive ears.

The bat receives information about the direction, loudness and pitch (high or low notes) of echoes returning from a flying insect. It can then work out the direction, distance and speed of the insect with amazing accuracy.

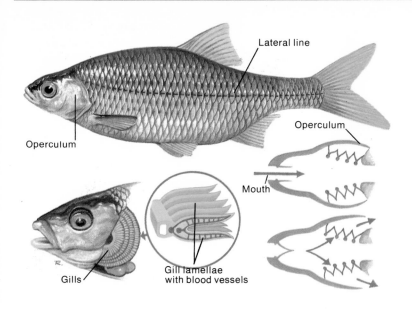

Lateral line

Operculum

Operculum

Mouth

Gills

Gill lamellae
with blood vessels

▲ HOW DO FISHES BREATHE?

A fish takes in oxygen through its gills. It causes water to flow over the gills and oxygen passes from the water into the gill blood vessels.

A fish's gills lie in two passages that lead from the back of the mouth cavity to the outside. Each of the openings to the outside is covered by a flap called the operculum.

Water is pumped over the gills. When the fish opens its mouth, the operculum is closed and the mouth cavity is expanded, drawing water in. Then the fish closes its mouth, the operculum is opened and the water is squeezed out over the gills.

The gills are supplied with many blood vessels that lie just beneath the surface of the skin. When water flows over the gills, oxygen is taken into the blood through the blood vessels and carbon dioxide is released into the water.

◄ HOW DO FISHES "SEE" WITH THEIR SIDES?

A fish has a special sensory system known as the lateral line system. This seems to provide the fish with information about what is going on around it.

The lateral line system of a fish consists of a canal down each side of the body that branches into several canals over the head. Inside each canal there is a row of neuromasts (groups of sensory cells), which have hairs running into the canal. In most fishes, the canals open to the surface by a long line of pores.

It is thought that neuromasts respond to pressure changes in the water around the fish. Using its lateral line system, a fish can tell that there are other fishes near it or even moving some distance away. This is useful in helping to detect prey or enemies. And it may help fishes that swim in shoals to stay together. It is also possible that the system helps a fish to detect objects by echo-location.

► HOW DOES A SPERM WHALE STAY UNDERWATER FOR LONG PERIODS?

A sperm whale can dive to a depth of about 3300 feet and may spend over an hour underwater. To achieve this it has to have very special control over its breathing and blood circulation.

In between deep dives, a sperm whale spends about ten minutes on the surface, taking between 60 and 70 breaths. With each breath it renews

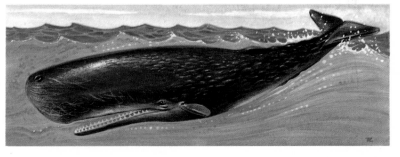

about nine-tenths of the air in its lungs. (Humans only renew about a quarter of the air.) Then, with its oxygen supply renewed, it dives again.

A whale is adapted in several ways to help it to stay underwater. For example, it

stores oxygen in its muscles. While diving, its heartbeat slows down and only essential organs, such as the brain and heart, are kept fully supplied with blood. The remaining organs have their blood supply reduced or cut off.

► HOW DOES A CATERPILLAR TURN INTO A BUTTERFLY?

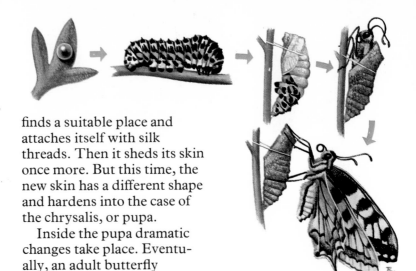

The amazing change from a caterpillar to a butterfly happens inside a chrysalis. The process is called metamorphosis, which means "change of form".

A caterpillar's life is spent feeding and growing. It eats large amounts of plant material. Every so often it sheds it skin, to show a larger skin underneath.

When it is fully grown, it finds a suitable place and attaches itself with silk threads. Then it sheds its skin once more. But this time, the new skin has a different shape and hardens into the case of the chrysalis, or pupa.

Inside the pupa dramatic changes take place. Eventually, an adult butterfly appears and flies away.

◄ HOW DOES A TADPOLE TURN INTO A FROG?

A tadpole becomes a frog by a series of dramatic changes. It develops lungs, grows legs, loses its tail and finally emerges from the water as a frog.

When a tadpole hatches from its egg, it has a small black body, a tail and a pair of feathery external gills. For a few days after hatching it has no mouth. It attaches itself to a leaf or a stone and feeds on the remains of its yolk.

Then it develops a mouth with a fringe of horny teeth and begins to feed by rasping off pieces of plant material. Soon afterwards it develops internal gills.

After about three months, metamorphosis, or a change of form, begins. The tadpole develops lungs and loses its internal gills. Then hind legs begin to develop and a few days later the front legs appear. The tail becomes shorter and the mouth gets bigger. Within a short time the animal has become a young frog.

► HOW DOES A CHICK HATCH OUT OF ITS EGG?

A chick usually has to break out of its shell by itself. To do this, it has a horny "egg tooth" on its beak and a "hatching muscle" on its neck.

When it is ready to hatch, a chick starts calling from inside the egg. This helps to make a bond between it and its parents. Within a few days it starts to chip away at the inside of the shell using its egg tooth. Then, using its strong hatching muscle, it heaves part of the shell away and struggles free. The egg tooth and hatching muscle disappear after a few days. Some birds usually take only a few hours to hatch. Larger birds may take up to three days.

Many chicks are helpless when they hatch out. They are often blind, naked and can only open their mouths for food. They may remain in the nest for several weeks.

Other birds, especially those that nest on the ground, have chicks that can run within a few days.

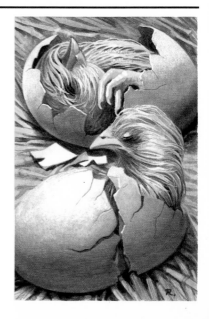

▶ HOW DOES A CAMEL CONSERVE WATER?

Camels are adapted to life in the desert. They save as much water as possible and they can also lose a lot of water without any bad effects.

Like all mammals, a camel has water in its body tissues. But it can lose up to 22 percent of this water without harm, while a human who has lost only 12 percent will almost certainly die. The camel can do this by losing most of the water from its body cells and very little from its blood. It looks rather scraggy, but a good drink of water brings it back to its normal appearance.

A camel's hump contains fat. This was once thought to be a source of water. But the fat is an energy reserve.

Camels do not sweat very much, and they produce only small amounts of urine. These adaptations help them to survive in the desert.

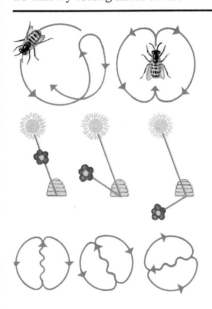

▲ HOW DOES A BEE TELL OTHERS WHERE TO FIND NECTAR?

When a bee finds a source of nectar (the bee's food), it returns to the hive and performs a waggle dance. This tells the other bees where the nectar is.

A honey bee performs its waggle dance on the surface of one of the vertical combs. Other bees cluster around to watch. If the bee is telling them of a nearby source of nectar, within about 50

yards, it performs a simple round dance (top left). The other bees then leave the nest to look for the food.

If the nectar source is far away, the bee performs a more complicated figure-eight dance (top right). The angle between the line of the straight run and the vertical shows the angle between the direction of the Sun and the direction of the food. So a vertical straight run means that the food lies in the same direction as the Sun. The other bees then know which way to fly to find the food.

◀ HOW DO BEES MAKE HONEY?

Bees gather nectar and pollen for food. Some of the nectar is converted into honey by the action of the bees' saliva.

A bees' nest is made up of a number of vertical wax sheets, or combs. On each side of a comb there are hundreds of small, six-sided cells. Some of these are used for rearing grubs and others are used for storing food.

An adult bee uses its long proboscis to suck up nectar, which supplies it with energy. Spare nectar is taken into its "honey stomach", brought back to the nest and stored in cells. The bee also gathers pollen, which it scrapes into two pollen baskets on its back legs. Pollen is a source of protein. It is also stored in cells and is fed to developing grubs.

Honey is also stored in cells as a winter food supply. Honey is not gathered from flowers. It is made by a bee sucking nectar into its crop. There, the action of saliva changes it into honey.

OURSELVES

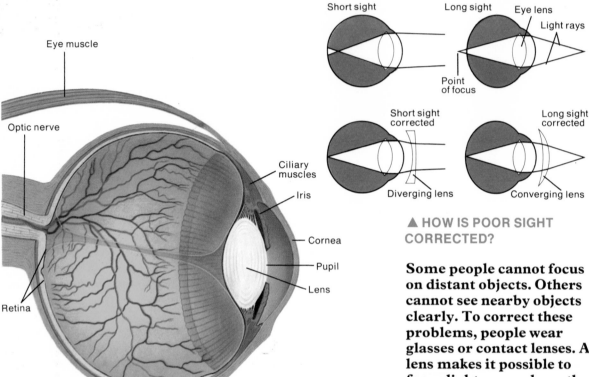

Eye muscle

Optic nerve

Retina

Ciliary muscles

Iris

Cornea

Pupil

Lens

Short sight

Long sight

Eye lens

Light rays

Point of focus

Short sight corrected

Long sight corrected

Diverging lens

Converging lens

▲ HOW IS POOR SIGHT CORRECTED?

Some people cannot focus on distant objects. Others cannot see nearby objects clearly. To correct these problems, people wear glasses or contact lenses. A lens makes it possible to focus light properly on the retina.

▲ HOW DO YOU SEE?

Your eye is a hollow ball filled with fluid. At the front there is a round hole that lets in light. This is focused onto light-sensitive cells at the back.

Light enters the eye through the transparent cornea and the hole, or pupil, in the center of the colored iris. The size of the pupil is automatically controlled by the muscles in the iris. The pupil shrinks in bright light and enlarges in dim light.

The ciliary muscles control focusing in the eye, and this alters the shape of the lens. When the eye focuses on an object far away, the lens is flattened. When it is a near object, the lens is more rounded.

At the back of the eye the light falls on the light-sensitive cells that form the retina. These send nerve impulses to the brain, which "sees" the picture that is formed at the back of the eye.

Muscles attached to the outside of your eyeball allow you to move your eyes. Having two forward-pointing eyes gives you stereoscopic vision and enables you to see three-dimensional images.

Short sight means that you cannot focus on far-away objects. It happens when the eyeball is longer than normal. Because of this, the retina lies behind the point at which light from distant objects is focused by the lens. To correct this, a short-sighted person uses lenses that diverge light rays before they enter the eye. Then they focus on the retina.

A long-sighted person cannot focus on nearby objects. In this case the eyeball is shorter than normal and the natural point of focus is behind the retina. To correct this, a converging lens that brings light rays together is used.

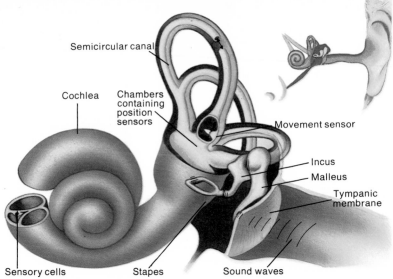

Semicircular canal

Cochlea

Chambers containing position sensors

Movement sensor

Incus

Malleus

Tympanic membrane

Sensory cells   Stapes   Sound waves

▲ HOW DO YOU HEAR?

Your ears are organs that convert sound waves into nerve impulses. Sound waves are passed from the outside to the cochlea. There, sensory cells are stimulated and send nerve impulses to the brain.

Sound waves cause the tympanic membrane to vibrate. The vibrations are passed on by three small bones called the malleus, incus and stapes.

The cochlea is a long, coiled tube filled with watery liquid. Vibrations pass from the stapes to the liquid and are picked up by a membrane in the middle of the cochlea. Sensory cells in this membrane are stimulated as it vibrates.

At the tip of the cochlea the membrane responds to low notes. Farther back, nearer the stapes, it responds to higher notes. Your brain senses exactly which sensory cells are being stimulated and "hears" the original sound.

◀ HOW DO YOU BALANCE?

The semicircular canals of your inner ear send information to your brain about the movements of your head.

Your inner ear contains three semicircular canals. Each one is set in a different plane and filled with liquid. Inside a swelling at one end of each canal there is a bunch of receptor cells. These have sensory hairs embedded in a lump of jelly-like material. When you move your head, the liquid in the semicircular canals causes the jelly-like lumps to shift and bend the sensory hairs. The receptor cells send the information to your brain.

Under the semicircular canals are two more chambers. Each of these contains another group of receptor cells with sensory hairs. But on the ends of these hairs are tiny chalky particles. These respond to gravity and the receptor cells send out information about the position of your head.

▶ HOW DO YOU TASTE AND SMELL THINGS?

Your nose and mouth contain special receptor cells. When these are stimulated by chemical molecules, they send nerve impulses to the brain.

Your tongue is covered with tiny lumps or papillae. On the sides of some papillae are small groups of cells known as taste buds. Each taste bud contains between four and 20 receptor cells with short sensory hairs. These react to molecules of food dissolved in your saliva.

Your tongue is sensitive to four main kinds of taste. Bitterness is tasted at the back of the tongue, sourness is tasted at the sides and sweetness is tasted at the front. Saltiness is tasted all over, especially at the tip.

Your smell receptors are in the roof of the nasal (nose) cavity. They have sensory hairs that branch and project into the mucus that lines the cavity. Molecules in the air dissolve in the mucus and stimulate these hairs. There are about 15 different kinds of smell receptors, and they can detect over 10,000 different smells.

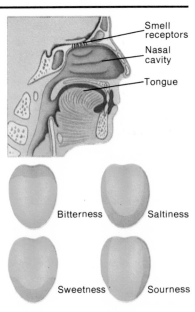

Smell receptors

Nasal cavity

Tongue

Bitterness   Saltiness

Sweetness   Sourness

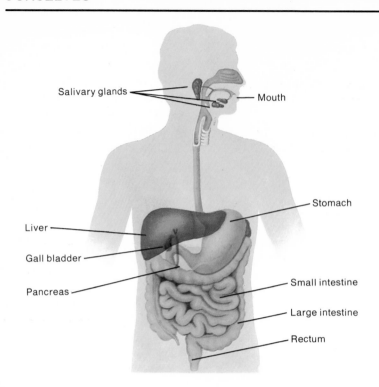

Salivary glands — Mouth

Liver —

Gall bladder —

Pancreas —

Stomach

Small intestine

Large intestine

Rectum

▲ HOW DO YOU DIGEST FOOD?

Your body digests food by breaking down compli-cated food chemicals into simpler ones. Digestion starts in the mouth and stomach, but most takes place in the small intestine.

Digestive juices contain enzymes, which are chemicals that help to break down food. Digestion begins in the mouth, where saliva mixes with food as it is chewed. Then the food is churned up in the stomach for some time.

There is some digestion in the stomach, but most happens in the small intestine. The churned-up food, or chyme, leaves the stomach a little at a time. In the small intestine it is mixed with bile (produced by the liver and stored in the gall bladder) and digestive juices from the pancreas. Proteins, carbo-hydrates and fats are broken down by enzymes into simple chemicals, which are then absorbed into the body.

The rest of the food passes into the large intestine. Water is taken back into the body. The remains, or faeces, go to the rectum.

◄ WHAT DOES YOUR LIVER DO?

The liver is the largest gland in the body. It receives all the food chemicals absorbed by the small intestine. The liver processes many of these chemicals.

Your liver works in many ways. It changes all carbohydrates into glucose and controls the amount of sugar in your blood by storing the excess as glycogen. It also helps with the processing of fats.

Amino acids are the product of protein digestion, and the body uses these to make new proteins. But excess amino acids cannot be stored, and so they are broken down by the liver into sugar and nitrogen-containing waste. The liver also makes certain proteins, such as the blood-clotting protein fibrinogen.

The liver makes bile, a greenish liquid which contains the remains of blood pigments collected by the liver from worn-out red blood cells. The liver also deals with any poisons in the blood, such as alcohol. The liver is also a storage organ. Iron, removed from blood pigment, is stored here as well as several vitamins.

► HOW DOES A STETHOSCOPE WORK?

A stethoscope is a device used for listening to sounds inside the body. The sounds are picked up at the surface of the body and transmitted along tubes to earpieces.

The first stethoscope was a wooden tube invented in 1815. The modern version was introduced in the late 1800s. Rubber tubes lead from a disk or cone to two earpieces. Sounds picked up by the cone are carried by the air in the tubes to the earpieces. This very simple device is still the easiest way of listening to a person's heart and lungs.

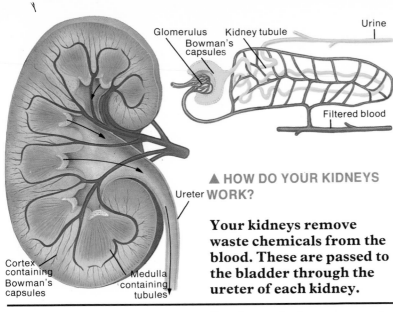

Glomerulus   Kidney tubule
Bowman's
capsules

Urine

Filtered blood

Cortex
containing
Bowman's
capsules

Medulla
containing
tubules

Ureter

▲ HOW DO YOUR KIDNEYS WORK?

Your kidneys remove waste chemicals from the blood. These are passed to the bladder through the ureter of each kidney.

A kidney consists of about two million microscopic filtering units. Each unit has a cup-shaped structure called a Bowman's capsule surrounding a tightly-bunched network of blood capillaries called a glomerulus.

Water and dissolved chemicals pass from the blood into the Bowman's capsule. Useful chemicals and over 80 percent of the water, are taken back into the blood from the tubule. Urine, containing waste chemicals, passes into the ureter.

▶ HOW DOES A KIDNEY MACHINE WORK?

If a person's kidneys do not work properly, waste chemicals build up in the blood. A special filtering device, or kidney machine, can take the place of the kidneys. Blood is pumped over a thin membrane that allows water and waste chemicals to pass through.

A person suffering from kidney failure is linked up to a kidney machine by two tubes.

One is attached to an artery in an arm. Blood from the artery is pumped into the machine.

Inside the machine the blood passes through a long tube that is made of a thin, semi-permeable plastic membrane. Outside the membrane is a salt solution that is kept well stirred. Water and dissolved waste chemicals pass through the membrane from the blood to the salt solution. The blood is then warmed and passed back to a vein in the person's arm. The process of cleaning the blood takes several hours.

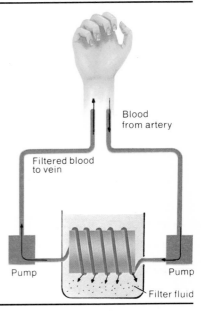

Blood
from artery

Filtered blood
to vein

Pump

Pump

Filter fluid

◀ HOW DO BONES MEND?

When a bone is broken, the two pieces must be held in place for several weeks so they can grow together properly. New bone material slowly forms between the pieces.

Bones may break, or fracture, in several different ways. A simple fracture is one in which the two ends remain in position, and not much damage is done to the surrounding tissue. In a compound fracture, the broken bone pierces the skin. In other kinds of fracture large blood vessels may be damaged, or the bone ends may be smashed.

The healing process begins when blood from broken blood vessels forms a clot. After a few days the broken ends of the bone become soft and the space between them fills with a sticky "glue" which contains bone-forming cells.

After two or three weeks, new soft bone tissue has completely filled the gap between the broken ends. This slowly hardens.

Simple fracture

Compound fracture

Complicated fracture

▶ HOW DO YOUR LUNGS WORK?

As you breathe in and out, your diaphragm contracts and relaxes, increasing and decreasing the volume of your lungs.

The movement of your lungs is controlled automatically by your diaphragm. When this muscular sheet contracts, it becomes flatter. When this happens, the pressure in the chest cavity is reduced and the lungs expand, drawing in air. At the same time the rib muscles contract, lifting the ribs upwards and outwards.

Breathing out takes place when the diaphragm and rib muscles relax. The lungs shrink and force the air out. A person's lungs contain between eight and twelve pints of air, but usually less than a pint is breathed in and out.

Air is breathed in through the mouth and nose. It passes into the windpipe, or trachea. This divides into two bronchi, which enter the lungs and divide into a number of smaller tubes called bronchioles. These divide into even smaller

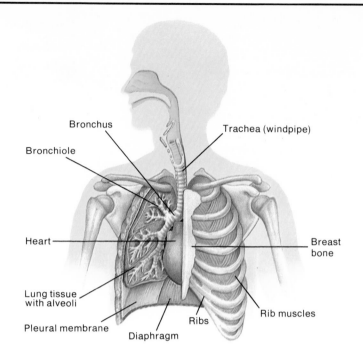

tubes, which finally end in tiny air sacs, or alveoli.

Each alveolus is surrounded by hundreds of minute blood vessels. The lining of the alveolus is very thin and is kept moist. Oxygen dissolves in the moisture and passes into the blood. Waste carbon dioxide passes from the blood into the alveoli and is breathed out.

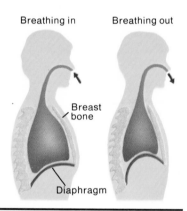

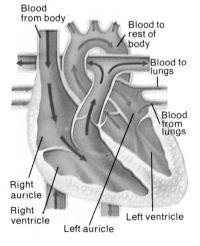

◀ HOW DOES YOUR HEART WORK?

Your heart is a muscular pump divided into two parts. One part pumps blood to your lungs. The other part pumps blood to the rest of the body.

Your heart consists of four chambers: two auricles and two ventricles. The walls of these chambers are made of special muscle that contracts rhythmically. Each heartbeat has two stages. The auricles contract first, followed

quickly by the ventricles. This gives your heartbeat its familiar "lub-dub" sound.

Between the chambers are one-way valves. These allow blood to flow through the chambers in one direction only. The right auricle receives blood from the body. As it contracts, blood flows into the right ventricle. When this contracts, it pumps the blood to the lungs.

The left auricle receives blood from the lungs and passes it to the left ventricle. This pumps blood to the rest of the body.

▶ HOW DOES A HEART-LUNG MACHINE WORK?

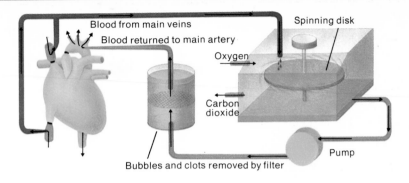

Blood from main veins
Blood returned to main artery
Oxygen
Spinning disk
Carbon dioxide
Pump
Bubbles and clots removed by filter

This machine is used during major heart surgery. The machine pumps blood around the body, supplies the blood with oxygen and removes carbon dioxide.

During a heart operation, the patient's heart cannot pump blood. And, because the chest cavity is open, the lungs cannot work either. So the main blood vessels are tied off and the patient's blood is piped into a heart-lung machine. There, oxygen is made to enter the blood. This is done either by bubbling oxygen through the blood in a bubble chamber, or (as shown here) by dripping the blood onto a spinning disk. There the blood forms a thin film into which oxygen can pass. Carbon dioxide is removed at the same time.

◀ HOW DO YOUR MUSCLES WORK?

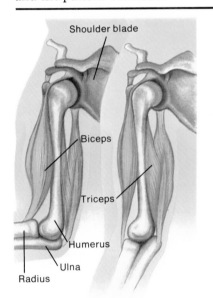

Shoulder blade
Biceps
Triceps
Humerus
Ulna
Radius

Muscles can only contract (shorten) and pull. So to move a part of your body to and fro, muscles have to act in pairs.

For every muscle that causes a particular movement, there is another muscle that causes an opposite movement. A typical example of this can be seen in the arm. To bend your arm at the elbow, you contract your biceps muscle. The top of this muscle is attached by tendons to your shoulder blade. The other end is attached to the radius bone of your forearm. When the biceps muscle contracts, your forearm is pulled towards the upper arm.

When you want to straighten your arm, your biceps muscle relaxes. But this by itself is not enough. The triceps muscle contracts, pulling on the back of the ulna bone, and the forearm swings downwards.

Other, more complicated movements involve using two opposing sets of muscles instead of just two muscles.

▶ HOW DOES A KNEE-JERK REFLEX HAPPEN?

When someone taps you just below the knee, you cannot stop your lower leg from jerking upwards. This is because the nerve impulses travel via the spinal cord directly to the leg muscle, and are not controlled by the brain.

When the tendon just below your knee-cap is given a sharp tap, the extensor muscle of your leg is slightly stretched. This stimulates a sensory nerve, which carries a nerve impulse to your spinal cord. Here, the sensory nerve divides and part of the impulse passes to the brain, telling the brain that the knee has been struck.

However, the brain does not control the knee's response. Part of the sensory impulse is sent directly to the motor nerve of the muscle.

To counteract the original stretching, the extensor muscle contracts. But it usually over-reacts, with the result that the leg jerks upwards.

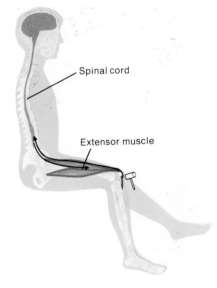

Spinal cord
Extensor muscle

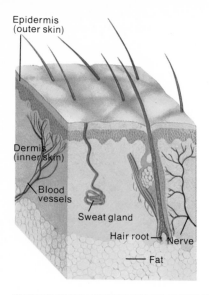

Epidermis (outer skin)

Dermis (inner skin)

Blood vessels

Sweat gland

Hair root — Nerve

— Fat

◄ WHAT IS YOUR SKIN FOR?

Your skin is a waterproof, elastic covering to your body. It helps to protect your body from damage and germs and also helps to keep your body at a constant temperature.

Your skin is a tough cushion that protects the tissues underneath. It acts as a barrier to germs and is also a sense organ, having receptors that respond to cold, heat, touch and pain. The skin makes vitamin D when exposed to sunlight and it produces hair and nails.

The skin is a waterproof body covering that prevents moisture from escaping. But moisture does escape through your sweat pores. This is particularly useful in hot conditions, as evaporating sweat cools you down. Cooling is also helped when blood vessels in the skin expand and heat is lost from the blood. In cold conditions, the surface blood vessels in the skin become narrower and help keep heat inside your body.

► WHAT ARE YOUR TEETH MADE OF?

A tooth consists of a crown above the gum and a root embedded in the bone of the jaw. A layer of hard enamel covers the crown. Under this outer enamel there is a layer of dentine surrounding the core, or pulp.

The outer layer of the crown of a tooth is made of a substance called enamel. This is the hardest substance in the body and is very resistant to wear. Inside the enamel layer is a layer of dentine. This is also hard, but not as hard as enamel. Dentine forms the roots (or just one root in the case of the front teeth), which are set into the jawbone with a layer of cement.

The inner core of the tooth is called the pulp. This contain nerve fibers and blood vessels. Nerve fibers also go through the dentine and cement layers. If the dentine is exposed by decay, painful toothache results. Cement left exposed by receding gums is also painful.

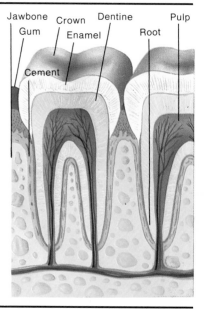

Jawbone Crown Dentine Pulp
Gum Enamel Root
Cement

◄ HOW DO YOUR TEETH WORK?

Your teeth consist of slicers, stabbers and grinders. The slicers (incisors) are at the front. Behind these are the stabbers, or canine teeth. At the back of the mouth are the grinders or molars. Children do not have as many teeth as adults.

Children have 20 teeth altogether. In each jaw there are four incisors. These are wedge-shaped teeth used for cutting off pieces of food. Behind the incisors are two pointed canine teeth, used for tearing off pieces of tough food that the incisors cannot cut. Behind the canines are four molars. These have broad, ridged crowns and are used for chewing food.

Adults have 32 teeth. They too have four incisors and two canine teeth in each jaw. But the molars they had as children have been replaced by four grinding premolars. In addition, adults have six molars at the back.

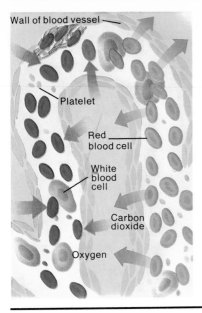

Wall of blood vessel

Platelet

Red blood cell

White blood cell

Carbon dioxide

Oxygen

◀ WHAT DOES YOUR BLOOD DO?

Blood is the vital transporting liquid of your body. It carries oxygen to all the tissues and takes carbon dioxide away to the lungs. It also carries food materials to the liver and other tissues and waste chemicals from the liver to the kidneys.

Blood consists of several kinds of cell suspended in a pale liquid called plasma. Over 55 percent of the blood is plasma, which is mostly water. Also in the plasma are proteins, minerals, food chemicals and waste chemicals.

There are three main kinds of cell in blood. Platelets are tiny cells that help in clotting. White blood cells fight disease. Red blood cells are the vital oxygen-carrying cells. There are many millions of them in the blood. They contain the red pigment hemoglobin, which picks up oxygen at the lungs and releases it into the tissues of the body.

▶ HOW DOES YOUR BLOOD HELP FIGHT DISEASE?

White blood cells are one of your body's main defense systems. There are several kinds. Some attack and engulf germs. Others help in producing special chemicals called antibodies.

Compared with the vast number of red blood cells, there are not many white blood cells in blood, only about 9000 in each cubic millimeter.

When germs invade the body, for example through a cut, white blood cells called neutrophils rush to the wound and begin to engulf the germs. Then larger white cells called monocytes appear and engulf more germs, together with any debris. Any germs that escape are dealt with by a third kind of white cell called lymphocytes. These recognize germs as being "foreign protein", or antigens. Then they start the production of antibodies, which are protein substances that stop germs working.

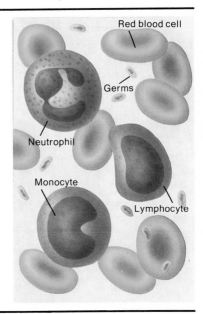

Red blood cell

Germs

Neutrophil

Monocyte

Lymphocyte

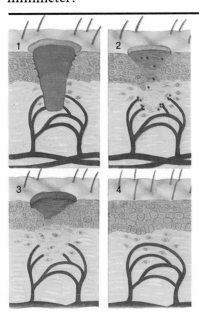

◀ HOW DOES A WOUND HEAL?

An open wound can be invaded by germs. To prevent infection, blood clots and forms a scab over the wound. New skin tissue develops beneath the scab.

When your skin is damaged, the broken blood vessels immediately become very narrow. This stops too much blood being lost and helps to keep germs out of the blood. Then substances released into the blood cause it to clot. The blood clot holds the edges of the wound together and hardens into a protective scab (1).

Meanwhile, white blood cells arrive at the wound and destroy dangerous bacteria (2). In the lower layer (the dermis) of the skin, special cells called fibroblasts move into the wound and start producing new tissue (2). In the upper layer (epidermis) the cells around the wound start to multiply and fill the gap (3). When this is nearly complete, the scab falls off (4).

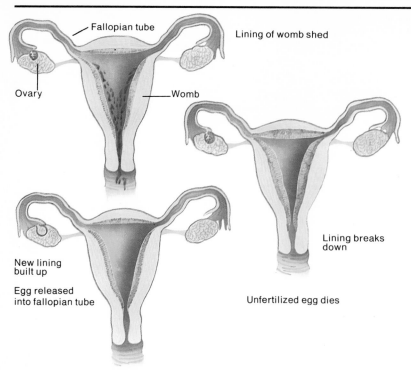

Fallopian tube

Lining of womb shed

Ovary

Womb

Lining breaks down

New lining built up

Egg released into fallopian tube

Unfertilized egg dies

▲ WHAT IS THE MENSTRUAL CYCLE?

This is the cycle of changes that occur in a woman as she produces eggs. The cycle takes about four weeks. During the first two weeks an egg develops in an ovary and is released into the womb. If it is not fertilized, it is expelled from the body with part of the womb lining.

At the start of the menstrual cycle an egg begins to ripen in one of the two ovaries. As it ripens, hormones are released into the body. These cause the womb to increase in size and its lining to thicken, ready for the egg to develop if it is fertilized.

After about 14 days the egg is released from the ovary and the womb continues to increase in size. If the egg is not fertilized on its way to the womb, it dies within two days. About a week later the womb begins to shrink and its lining breaks down.

On the last day of the cycle the unfertilized egg and the remains of the womb lining are expelled, together with some blood. This process is called menstruation and it lasts for about five days. Menstruation begins some time between the ages of 12 and 14. It continues until the age of about 50.

▶ WHAT CAUSES TWINS?

Identical twins occur when a single fertilized egg splits into two. Both cells then develop into a baby. Non-identical twins are the result of two separate eggs being fertilized at the same time.

If a fertilized egg splits into two, both cells start to develop in the normal way. They become implanted in the womb close together and, as a result, both developing babies share the same placenta.

Identical twins are of the same sex. They share the same features, such as hair color, height and weight and look very much alike. Non-identical twins develop from two separate eggs fertilized at

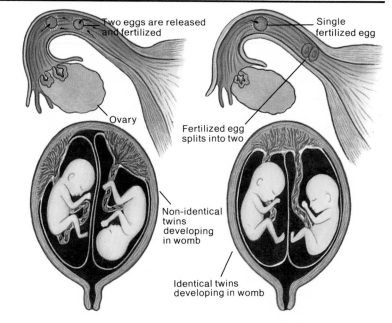

Two eggs are released and fertilized

Single fertilized egg

Ovary

Fertilized egg splits into two

Non-identical twins developing in womb

Identical twins developing in womb

the same time. In the womb they are nourished by separate placentas. They may or may not be of the same sex and they bear no more than a family likeness to each other.

Non-identical twins are born more often than identical twins. Triplets are usually a combination of identical twins and a non-identical brother or sister.

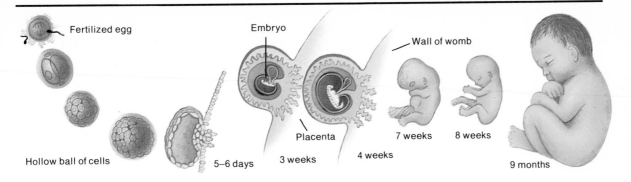

Fertilized egg

Embryo

Wall of womb

Placenta

7 weeks

8 weeks

Hollow ball of cells

5–6 days

3 weeks

4 weeks

9 months

▲ HOW DOES A BABY DEVELOP?

A baby begins life as a fertilized egg. This develops quickly into an embryo. After eight weeks it is recognizable as a human baby. It continues to grow and after nine months it is born.

After about nine days a fertilized egg has developed into a hollow ball of cells, which becomes implanted in the wall of the womb. Part of this ball, with part of the womb lining, forms the placenta. This is the organ that keeps the developing embryo supplied with food and oxygen. The major organs of the embryo, such as the heart and brain, appear soon. After about six weeks the limbs, eyes and ears develop.

After eight weeks the baby (now called a fetus) has almost all its organs and tissues, including its nervous system, muscles and skeleton. During the next seven months all these continue to develop.

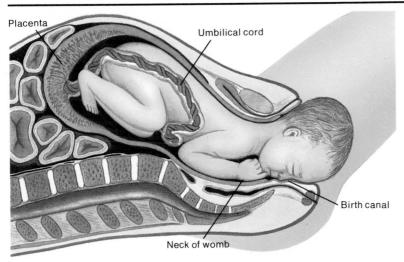

Placenta

Umbilical cord

Birth canal

Neck of womb

▲ HOW IS A BABY BORN?

When a baby is ready to be born, the mother begins labor. The muscles of the womb push the baby downwards and the neck of the womb starts to open. Eventually, the baby is pushed out.

Labor appears to start because the baby has reached the right stage of development. Labor pains are contractions of the womb. These may continue for several hours, gradually becoming stronger and more frequent. All the time the baby's head is being pushed down, gradually stretching the neck of the womb. When the neck of the womb is fully open, the membranes around the baby break, releasing fluid (this sometimes happens earlier). Then the baby is pushed out.

Soon after it is born, the baby begins to breathe and the umbilical cord is cut. Then the afterbirth (the placenta and membranes) is also pushed out.

◄ WHAT IS A TEST-TUBE BABY?

Babies do not grow in test-tubes! A so-called "test-tube baby" is produced by removing an egg from a woman's ovary and fertilizing it outside her body. The fertilized egg is then placed inside the womb, where it grows.

Some women cannot have children in the normal way. The woman's fallopian tubes (the tube leading from the ovaries to the womb) may be blocked, or the man's sperm may not be fertile enough.

In such cases, doctors can perform an operation to remove one of the woman's eggs. The egg is placed in a special culture material, where it is fertilized with sperm taken from the man. The fertilized egg starts to divide in the usual way. When the embryo is still just a ball of cells, it is inserted into the woman's womb. There it grows into a normal baby.

INDEX

Page numbers in *italics* refer to pictures

PHOTOGRAPHIC ACKNOWLEDGEMENTS

Pages: 14 Zefa, 19 Picturepoint, 20, 21, 23, & 31 J. Allan Cash, 33 Fiat, 34 J. Allan Cash, 38 Zefa, 41 Rank Xerox, 42 Zefa, 44 Rose-Morris & Co. Ltd., 47 Michael Holford, 54 David Oliver, 57 J. Allan Cash, 61 Ferranti, 63 B.S.C., 65 Pat Morris, 66 top Bell Inc., 66 bottom California Institute of Technology, 70 Heather Angel, 73 Zefa, 77 J. Allan Cash, 78 Zefa, 80 Zefa, 85 National Radio Astronomy, 89 Nasa, 93 Nasa, 95 top Meteorological Office, 95 center Nasa, 96 Nasa, 106 Zefa, 116 Picturepoint.

Picture Research: Penny Warn and Jackie Cookson.